Rethinking the Haitian Revolution

Slavery, Independence, and the Struggle for Recognition

Alex Dupuy
Wesleyan University

ROWMAN & LITTLEFIELD
Lanham • Boulder • New York • London

Published by Rowman & Littlefield
An imprint of The Rowman & Littlefield Publishing Group, Inc.
4501 Forbes Boulevard, Suite 200, Lanham, Maryland 20706
https://rowman.com

6 Tinworth Street, London SE11 5AL, United Kingdom

British Library Cataloguing in Publication Information Available

Library of Congress Cataloging-in-Publication Data
Names: Dupuy, Alex, author.
Title: Rethinking the Haitian Revolution : slavery, independence, and the struggle for recognition / Alex Dupuy, Wesleyan University.
Description: Lanham, MD : Rowman & Littlefield, [2019] | Includes bibliographical references and index.
Identifiers: LCCN 2018055317 (print) | LCCN 2018056427 (ebook) | ISBN 9781442261129 (ebook) | ISBN 9781442261105 (cloth : alk. paper) | ISBN 9781442261112 (pbk. : alk. paper)
Subjects: LCSH: Haiti—History—Revolution, 1791–1804—Influence. | Haiti—History—Revolution, 1791–1804—Economic aspects. | Slavery—Economic aspects—Haiti. | Slavery—Haiti—History—18th century. | Slaves—Emancipation—Haiti—History. | Indemnity—France—History. | Haiti—Economic conditions—19th century. | Social classes—Haiti. | Haiti—Relations—France. | France—Relations—Haiti.
Classification: LCC F1923 (ebook) | LCC F1923 .D87 2019 (print) | DDC 972.94/03—dc23
LC record available at https://lccn.loc.gov/2018055317

Printed in the United States of America

To Wanda

Contents

Foreword

Robert Fatton Jr.

I am honored to write the foreword for this new book by my dearest colleague and friend, Alex Dupuy. Dupuy is one of those rare social scientists whose work consistently "speaks the truth to power" uncovering and demystifying the ugly structures of oppression. In his analysis of Haitian history, he has no patience with those forms of nationalism that hide the domestic sources of exploitation while exclusively blaming external causes for the country's past and current predicament. This is not to say that Alex ignores the negative role played by imperial interferences in Haiti's economy and politics, but rather that he underscores the ways in which such intrusions were welcomed by Haitian rulers in defense of their own corporate interests. In short, Haitian history has always been marked by an opportunistic convergence of interests between privileged domestic actors and powerful external agents.

Rethinking the Haitian Revolution: Slavery, Independence, and the Struggle for Recognition, like much of Alex's work, is grounded in a spirit of opposition and critique rather than accommodation. It represents an inspiration to those of us who believe that the challenge of the intellectual life is to be found in dissent against the status quo at a time when social science is increasingly becoming an apology for the dominant order. His study is informed by a profound humanism and empathy for those who suffer the ravages of exploitation.

Rethinking the Haitian Revolution offers a succinct and sophisticated analysis of the roles played by slavery, race, and class in the history of Haiti. Dupuy examines their complicated interconnections to explain the triumphs and failures of both the Haitian Revolution and the vicissitudes of the country's political economy. He renews an old debate about the slave mode of production and its integration into the world capitalist economy. While he shows that slavery—a most cruel and brutal form of unpaid labor—generated an extremely productive sugar economy in Haiti during the early phases of world capitalist expansion, he argues convincingly that as capitalism matured, slavery and its legacy became obstacles to technological innovation and eventually curbed the development of an independent Haiti, and the Caribbean more broadly. Moreover, Dupuy critically examines how the Western Enlightenment, quintessentially distilled in the writings of Georg Wilhelm Friedrich Hegel, secreted a racist ideology that legitimated the exploitative slave plantation system. Contrary to certain contemporary interpretations of Hegel's views, Dupuy argues forcefully that the master-slave relationship in Saint-Domingue was never one of mutual recognition. It was in fact a life-and-death struggle between two antagonistic actors that ended in a bloody slave revolution and the creation of an independent Haiti.

Haiti's Revolution of 1804 represented a radical rupture with the white supremacist order of the time. It carried the egalitarian hopes of abolishing race as a marker of oppression and thus embodied a profoundly significant moment in world history. The revolution was, however, inhibited by both that very global order, and the intense processes of domestic class formation. In spite of these international constraints, Haitian rulers enjoyed a relative degree of autonomy in molding their patterns of governance; like all their counterparts in the world, they sought to advance their own class interests. Dupuy challenges the conventional wisdom that attributes many of Haiti's early political and economic problems to the so-called indemnity debt forced on Haiti by the French government in 1825. In the face of French military threats, the Haitian regime of Jean-Pierre Boyer agreed to pay an indemnity of 150 million francs to France in return for its recognition of Haiti's independence. Dupuy does not downplay the raw power of French imperialism in Haiti's decision to pay the indemnity, nor does he suggest that the debt had no negative effects on the future development of the country, but he does insist convincingly that Boyer's decision was largely determined by the class interests he represented. As Dupuy puts it, Boyer and the members of the ruling class "believed that the 'property question'—i.e., the properties of the former colonial owners that the revolutionary governments from Toussaint Louverture to Jean-Pierre Boyer confiscated and redistributed to create a new landed bourgeoisie in Haiti—could be resolved." In short, Haitian rulers were determined to secure their newly acquired ownership of the land against any potential imperial encroachments by ensuring that France would recognize Haiti's national sovereignty and thus respect its property laws. In addition, they assumed—and rightly so—that once France had recognized Haiti's independence, other major powers would follow.

Finally, Dupuy contends that what really prevented the economic development of Haiti was the incapacity of the Haitian ruling class to impose its hegemony over society in any systematic way. In other words, this class's continuing fragility and internecine conflicts blocked whatever meaningful economic and political projects it might have wanted to enact. It is true that such intraclass wranglings were, and still are, nurtured by imperial interventions in the domestic affairs of the country. Yet the reality is that Haiti's ruling class has always lacked the material, ideological, and political attributes that have characterized classical bourgeoisies. It is unproductive, dependent, parasitic, and opportunistic.

Rethinking the Haitian Revolution is insightful and provocative; it represents an important scholarly intervention in Haitian and Caribbean studies. It offers new theoretical insights to understand how the interactions among slavery, race, and class produced patterns of underdevelopment that, in turn, were exacerbated by both an unrelenting white supremacist world order and the contradictions of Haiti's own ruling class. The legacy of this order and these contradictions has been a constant burden on Haiti's development. This book does not pretend to offer an easy way out of this quandary, but it explains its roots.

This is not to imply that there is no hope; in fact, as the Haitian Revolution shows, even in the most oppressive conditions, human beings are capable of taking matters into their own hands to express triumphantly their moral outrage at injustice. The slaves of Saint-Domingue mustered the energy and courage to challenge the harsh realities of their subordination; they expanded the boundaries of the possible and generated one of those rare moments of human liberation. Dupuy's work captures well these moments, but it also shows their limitation. He explains persuasively how they often fail to bring about the social transformations they promise. *Rethinking the Haitian Revolution* gives us the required conceptual tools with which to understand the shortcomings of both Haiti's emancipation and its more than two centuries of political development.

Acknowledgments

I am very grateful to my wife, Wanda Dupuy, for her invaluable assistance during the summer of 2014 for digitizing and cataloging documents from the National Archives, Kew, Richmond, England; the Archives Nationales, Paris and Pierrefite-sur-Seine; the Ministère des Affaires Étrangères, Paris; and the Archives Nationales d'Outre-Mer, Aix-en-Provence, France; and for her support and encouragement in writing this book.

I am also very grateful to my very dear friend and kindred spirit Robert Fatton Jr. for doing me the honor of writing the foreword and for his thoughtful comments and suggestions on the chapters of this book.

I thank my friend and colleague Gina Ulysse for suggesting the title *Rethinking the Haitian Revolution*.

I would also like to thank Susan McEachern, vice president and senior executive acquisitions editor, Rowman & Littlefield, for her editorial suggestions and her support at every stage and iteration of this project.

Author Note

Unless otherwise noted, all translations from French or Haitian Kreyòl texts in this book are my own.

Chapter 3, "From Saint-Domingue to Haiti: Revolution and the Rise of a New Bourgeoisie," is a revised version of the article "Class, Race, and Nation: Unresolved Contradictions of the Saint-Domingue Revolution," originally published in the *Journal of Haitian Studies* 10, no. 1 (Spring 2004): 6–21. Reprinted with permission.

Introduction

In the eleventh of the "Theses on Feuerbach," Marx wrote that "philosophers have only interpreted the world, in various ways; the point is to change it" (Marx 1977, 158). In 1791 the slaves in the French colony of Saint-Domingue took up arms to change the world they were living in. But they did not do so after they had written theses or manifestos to interpret that world. They left that task to those philosophers on both sides of the Atlantic who either sought to justify and preserve that world or believed it was unjust and needed to be changed. For their part, the slaves who revolted in August of that year had concluded long before that the world into which they had been forced and kept in chains was not fit for human beings. Their uprising was not new but followed a long succession of revolts that started in 1516 when the indigenous Taino population revolted against the Spanish colonialists who had first conquered the island they renamed Hispaniola. But the key difference between all the uprisings from 1516 to 1791 was that the latter became a full-blown revolution that would transform the slave system and replace it with a new social order that became the independent Republic of Haiti in 1804.

The four chapters that follow, however, consist of interpreting the world created by French imperialism in the colony of Saint-Domingue in the seventeenth century and the one created by Haiti's new ruling classes after they won independence from France in 1804. Saint-Domingue became the most productive and wealthiest slave economy in the Caribbean in the eighteenth century until the slave uprising of 1791 destroyed it. The revolutionary government then declared the colony's independence and renamed it Haiti, but France refused to recognize that independence until Haiti's leaders agreed to pay an indemnity to compensate the former colonial masters for the loss of their properties. The themes that connect the four chapters, then, are slavery, revolution, independence, and the struggle for the recognition of the new nation.

Chapter 1, "Capitalism and Slavery: Revisiting an Old Debate," reconsiders the differing views, including my own, on the relationship between capitalism and slavery and the role the latter played in the processes of uneven development of capitalism in western Europe and the Caribbean since the sixteenth century. There are two key issues that need to be clarified. One is theoretical and has to do with the definition of capitalism. The other is methodological and empirical and has to do with the difference between the abstract definition of capitalism and its actual development in space and time.

Theoretically, the debate consisted of two opposing arguments. On one side were those who defined capitalism as an economic system based on free wage-labor for the production of commodities for sale in a market for profit (surplus value). They, therefore, did not consider slavery as a capitalist social relation of production even if the slaves produced commodities for sale in a market for profit. Moreover, those who took that view also argued that the wage-labor system enabled capitalists to develop productive forces by constantly innovating and introducing new technology in the production process, substituting machinery for labor while increasing the exploitation of labor and the accumulation of capital. Thus, from that perspective, the processes of uneven development in the world economy are to be explained by the degree to which wage-labor becomes generalized in a particular economy to make possible the development of the productive forces and the production of commodities for both the domestic economy and the world market.

In contrast to those who saw the wage-labor social relation as the *sine qua non* of capitalism, there were others who defined capitalism as a world-system for the production of commodities for sale in a market for profit. But that system comprised a tripartite international division of labor among core, semi-peripheral, and peripheral countries, each with different relations of production or forms of labor control, such as a predominance of wage-labor in the core; a combination of wage- and semi-wage-labor in the semi-periphery; and slavery or other forms of coerced labor, cash-crop production, and a minimum of wage-labor in the periphery. In addition to being able to develop their productive forces because of the preponderance of wage-labor relations in the core in contrast to the peripheral countries, the former also accumulated capital in the world economy as a whole by appropriating the surpluses produced in the semi-peripheral and peripheral countries. Thus, uneven geographic development resulted not only from the different relations and modes of labor exploitation in the different zones of the world-system, but also from the exploitation of the semi-periphery and the periphery by the core.

My own earlier views on the relationship between capitalism and slavery coincided with those I included in the first group of theorists. I now offer a different argument that combines elements of both perspectives outlined above. I draw on Marx's methodology to distinguish between the abstract definition of capitalism as predicated on the capital-wage-labor relations and its actual development in space and time since its emergence in the sixteenth century. Marx defined capitalism as a social system of production of commodities for sale in a market for profit that required the existence of capitalists who owned the means of production and capital, on the one hand, and, on the other hand, wage-laborers (proletarians) who, deprived of access to their own means of production, were compelled to sell their labor-power to the capitalists in return for a wage in order to live. Marx, therefore, based his analysis of the modus operandi of that system on the existence of the capitalist-wage-labor relations.

But Marx also showed that the actual historical development of that system and its processes of capital accumulation rested on different forms of labor relations in different parts of the world economy created by the expanding western European colonial powers since the sixteenth century. One such system of labor created for the sole purpose of producing commodities (e.g., sugar, cotton, coffee, indigo) for the world market for profit was that of slavery established in the New World colonies of the Americas. Such was the case in the French colony of Saint-Domingue, which became the most productive and wealthiest of all the colonies in the Caribbean in the eighteenth century. At the same time, as productive as it was, the slave system in Saint-Domingue, or in any other Caribbean colony such as Cuba in the nineteenth century, prevented the development and innovation of the productive forces by substituting machinery for labor. That is why, despite the enormous wealth they produced, the slave economies of the Caribbean remained undeveloped. In the context of the world economy created by the western European colonial powers, therefore, slavery in the New World colonies must be understood as capitalist because its only reason for being was to produce commodities for profit for the slave masters, the metropolitan economies, and the world market.

Chapter 2, "Masters, Slaves, and Revolution in Saint-Domingue: A Critique of the Hegelian Interpretation," draws on the argument developed in the first chapter on the capitalist characteristics of the system of racial slavery created by French imperialism in the seventeenth century to offer a critique of the arguments advanced by Pierre-Franklin Tavares, Susan Buck-Morss, and Nick Nesbitt that Hegel derived his iconic master-slave "life-and-death struggle" dialectic in the *Phenomenology of Mind* from the 1791 Saint-Domingue Revolution.

In contrast to these three authors, who do not provide substantive evidence to support their claims, I offer two reasons why Hegel could not have done so. The first has to do with Hegel's racist views of history and of Africans as savages who have never evolved from the state of nature. As such, although he believed that slavery in general was unjust, he justified the enslavement of Africans in the New World colonies as a means of raising them above their savagery and argued that their gradual emancipation was far more desirable than doing so suddenly. He thus a priori ruled out a slave revolution as a meaningful path to freedom.

Second, in the *Phenomenology* Hegel depicted the master and the slave as engaging in a "life-and-death" struggle for recognition. But realizing that they could not kill one another, they "sublate" their extreme terms in such a way that the one combatant who was willing to risk his life became the master, and the other, who feared death, became the slave. Hegel understood that relationship as one of domination and inequality, but he also saw it as one of mutual dependence between the master and the slave. The latter recognized the master, but the master, though dependent on the slave, did not recognize him as an equal. The slave, then, came to realize that it was through his labor that he would obtain both his freedom from and recognition by the master.

I argue, however, that in the real world of racial slavery in Saint-Domingue, the master-slave relation was not one where master and slave sought mutual recognition. As I demonstrate in the first chapter, the slave system was predicated on the brutal exploitation of the slaves by the master to extract the maximum profit from them in the shortest time possible. For their part, the slaves knew that they would not obtain their freedom through labor, but only by getting rid of the master. It was indeed a life-and-death struggle, but one where this time the slaves were willing to risk their lives, did so, and emerged victorious. Moreover, I argue, the slaves were not fighting only to free themselves from their masters but to create a different social order where they would be the masters of their own labor and destiny. The radicalness of the Saint-Domingue/Haitian Revolution, then, was that it sought to end not only the system of slavery but that of class exploitation in general. The subsequent two chapters analyze those struggles and their outcomes.

Chapter 3, "From Saint-Domingue to Haiti: Revolution and the Rise of a New Bourgeoisie," expands on the argument on the class and racial system of Saint-Domingue before the slave revolution of 1791 developed in the previous two chapters, to show how a new indigenous class system and ideologies of color and divisions emerged during the revolution when the government of Toussaint Louverture took control of the colony in 1800. The Saint-Domingue Revolution challenged the premises of the colonial, slave-based, and white supremacy system by declaring once and for all that the ideals of liberty, equality, justice, and self-determination championed by the preceding American and French revolutions belonged to all of humanity and not only to white European and American men.

But though it challenged the ideology of white supremacy and abolished the system of chattel slavery, the Saint-Domingue Revolution gave rise to new class formations and ideologies of color that would characterize the emerging nation of Haiti before and after it declared its independence in 1804. On the one hand, the revolution, started by slaves whose objectives were to abolish slavery and create a more egalitarian society of independent and landowning farmers, was taken over by its leaders when they took control of the colony in 1800. Their objective was to become the new rulers of the colony, take over the properties of the colonial planter class, and preserve the colonial plantation system by turning the former slaves into free wage-laborers. It is in this sense that I argue that the revolution was transformed into a bourgeois revolution.

The emerging ruling class, however, was divided between the old property-owning *affranchis*—commonly referred to as "free people of color" because of the predominance of mulattoes among them—and the black faction that came to control the colonial state under the leadership of Toussaint Louverture in 1800 and began to acquire properties belonging to the colonial planter class who had fled the colony. The conflicts between these two factions of the new ruling class expressed themselves primarily in terms of ideologies of color that embodied elements of the ideology of white supremacy of the colonial and slave era but were not mere replicas of it. They became more fluid in terms of individual classification and correlated more or less with class position such that those of lighter skin complexion tended to be found more among the dominant and wealthier classes than among the poorer and more powerless. Those ideologies of color would become integral to the conflicts between the two principal ruling class factions comprising blacks and mulattoes for control of the state and the economy in post-colonial Haiti.

Chapter 4, "Property, Debt, and Development: Rethinking the Indemnity Question," reconsiders the widely held belief that in 1825 under the presidency of Jean-Pierre Boyer Haiti was forced, under the threat of military action, to pay an indemnity of 150 million francs to France in return for its recognition of Haiti's independence. It is also known that Boyer subsequently succeeded in reducing that original amount to 60 million francs. But since Haiti had borrowed 30 million francs from a French banking consortium to make the first payment on the 150 million, the total amount that Haiti had to pay to France came to 90 million plus interest. Many of those who hold that view also argued that the crushing indemnity was largely responsible for Haiti's inability to develop its economy in the nineteenth century and beyond.

Contrary to these views, I offer a different argument that focuses on the class interests that Boyer, and President Alexandre Pétion before him, were defending when they offered to pay an indemnity to France in return for its recognition of Haiti's independence. No doubt, the international context, especially the diplomatic isolation of Haiti due to the refusal of the other major imperialist Western powers to recognize its independence before France did so, played an important role in their decisions. But, as I showed in chapter 3, the revolutionary government of Toussaint Louverture had created a new landowning class alongside the old property-owning class comprising the free people of color by seizing the properties of the former colonial owners and redistributing them to higher-ranking military officers and government officials. That process continued under the governments of Jean-Jacques Dessalines (1804–1806), Henri Christophe (1806–1820), Alexandre Pétion (1808–1818), and Jean-Pierre Boyer (1818–1843). Thus, I argue, Boyer, as had Pétion before him, believed that resolving the "property question"—that is, the properties of the former colonial owners that had been confiscated and redistributed to create a new landed bourgeoisie in Haiti since Louverture—was the *conditio sine qua non* of recognition and the indemnity was the price to pay to achieve it.

I also offer two arguments against the view that the indemnity was a major reason that Haiti could not develop its economy in the nineteenth century. The first focuses on the inability of the dominant classes to proletarianize the peasants to revitalize the sugar plantations that had been the basis of Saint-Domingue's immense wealth in the eighteenth century. On the one hand, the failure to create such a proletariat compelled the dominant classes to accommodate themselves to the new class configurations that comprised a majority of landowning peasants, tenant farmers, and sharecroppers to produce the commodities Haiti exported on the world market (coffee, cotton, indigo, cacao, lumber). This also meant, on the other hand, that the landed bourgeoisie would derive its wealth primarily from the rents extracted from the tenant farmers and sharecroppers, the buying and selling of the cash crops the farmers produced on the world market, and importing and reselling commodities on the domestic market. Thus, notwithstanding these new class configurations, Haiti remained fully integrated in the capitalist world economy because the raw materials and agricultural and other commodities it produced for the world market, and the surplus value contained in them, entered the circuits of industrial and financial capital in the advanced countries.

The second reason Haiti could not develop its economy in the nineteenth century had to do with the perpetual internecine conflicts among different factions of the post-independence ruling class since Dessalines's assassination in 1806 to control the state to use it as a means of social promotion and wealth accumulation. As such, the state could not use its authority or its resources to promote or coordinate economic development. The weakness, divisions, and conflicts among the factions of the ruling class opened them to being manipulated or exploited by foreign governments and their business classes to reassert their influence and eventually their dominance over Haiti's governments and economy. The invasion and occupation of Haiti by the United States from 1915 to 1934 represented the major turning point in foreign capital's return to and dominance over Haiti.

The theoretical threads that run through these chapters, then, are as follows. The first has to do with how one understands the relationship between capitalism, wage-labor, slavery, non-wage-labor, and the processes of uneven economic development in the world economy created by the major western European colonial powers since the sixteenth century. The argument here is to show that while slavery must be seen as a capitalist relation of production and could be the basis for a highly productive economy, it also imposed severe limits on technological and industrial development in contrast to an economy based on free-wage labor.

The second deals with the class and racial/color hierarchies slavery generated in the colony and how they determined the relations among masters, slaves, and those in between who came to be known as free people of color, commonly referred to as mulattoes. My main task here is to explain why, after having waged a successful revolution, a new class system was created. It comprised two characteristics. On the one hand a division emerged between the rulers of the revolutionary government who became a new property-owning class and the former slaves. And on the other hand, it pitted the new, predominantly black landowning class against the old, predominantly mulatto property-owning class, to determine who would control the state after independence.

And the third is to explain why, after the revolution destroyed the slave system, the new dominant classes of Haiti were unable to develop the economy. Two arguments are offered to account for that outcome. One has to do with the divisions between the dominant factions of the new ruling class based largely on a reformulation of the ideologies of color inherited from the colonial era and their struggles to control the state. And the second was the inability of these warring factions to proletarianize the former slaves and their descendants, thus making them unable to create the conditions for a sustainable process of economic development in the nineteenth century. I maintain, however, that, on the basis of the arguments developed in chapters 1 and 4 in particular, one must understand the production relations in post-independent Haiti characterized mostly by landowning farmers, rent-paying tenant farmers, and sharecroppers producing cash crops and agricultural and other raw materials for both the domestic and world markets as capitalist insofar as the Haitian economy and its class relations were embedded in the processes of commodity production, capital accumulation, and commercial relations of the wider capitalist world economy.

Chapter One

Capitalism and Slavery

Revisiting an Old Debate

My objective in this chapter is to analyze and clarify the relationship between capitalism and slavery in the French colony of Saint-Domingue in the seventeenth and eighteenth centuries. Essentially, I will argue, the creation of the slave-based economy in the Taino island of Ayiti in the sixteenth century was not an inevitable outcome of colonialism but became a necessary alternative once the Spanish annihilated the indigenous population and could not find alternative sources of labor from Spain for the sugar plantations it had established there. It first tried enslaving indigenous peoples from neighboring islands, but quickly turned to importing slaves from Africa, where the Portuguese had been involved in the slave trade since the middle of the fifteenth century. France conquered the western third of the island in the seventeenth century, named it Saint-Domingue, and quickly transformed it into the most productive and wealthiest slave economy in the Caribbean in the eighteenth century. The colony was renamed Haiti after the only successful slave revolution (1791–1804) in the world led to creation of the second independent republic (after the United States) in the New World.

Historians and other social theorists working out of the Marxist tradition in the Caribbean and Haiti have grappled with the role that European colonialism and slavery played in the development of capitalism since the sixteenth century. For example, in his seminal *Capitalism and Slavery* (1966), the historian Eric Williams[1] argues that slavery in the Caribbean was a direct consequence of the development of capitalism in western Europe for the

1

purpose of facilitating the accumulation of capital in the metropolitan countries. Sidney Mintz also argues that although New World slavery was admit-
tedly different than the free wage-labor system of western European capitalism in several respects, it cannot be understood outside of the context of the
global capitalist world economy that spawned it and of which it was an
integral part. Here, Mintz was invoking Immanuel Wallerstein's argument,
which I will discuss below, that it is the "relations of production of the world
system" as a whole that define and give meaning to the social relations in a
particular area of the world-economy (Mintz 1978, 97). Likewise, Clive
Thomas pointed out that the plantation system created in the Caribbean was a
capitalist institution that was created by and dependent on the development
of capitalism on a world scale. It was not a "separate 'mode of production'
[that] grew out of the communal or slave forms of production which pre-
ceded it, nor was it derived from the feudal origins of Europe" (Thomas
1988, 22–23).

In the case of Saint-Domingue more specifically, Gérard Pierre-Charles
argues that its colonization was the Antillean creation of western European
mercantilism. But it was the vigorous development of capitalism in France
during the eighteenth century that called for the large-scale development of
colonial production based on slave labor. Thus,

> under conditions of colonial domination, exercised by a European power in
> full capitalist expansion, the organization of production in Saint-Domingue,
> while slavery in form, was capitalist in its origin and in its content. The
> production of commodities for the capitalist world market constituted the su-
> preme motivation of the system. (Pierre-Charles 1972, 23)

Nonetheless, Pierre-Charles qualified his views of slavery as fully capitalist.[2] The cycle of production in slavery, he argues, corresponded to the capitalist process of money-commodity-money (M-C-M'), which Marx called
the "general formula for capital." The money invested in slave production
(M) came from the metropole, and the money increased by its profit (M')
was destined for the metropole. Yet, in the relations of production on the
plantations, there existed a category that was

> atypical of capitalism, proper to an archaic socio-economic formation: a ser-
> vile labor force. Under conditions of world mercantilism, it was identified as a
> commodity, a property. In its form, it was not reproducible as was the labor-
> er—by the wage. In its essence, it was reproducible by a renewal through
> purchase, which granted it a commodity content. (Pierre-Charles 1972, 7)

Mintz also clarified his views on slavery-as-capitalist. Unlike proletarians, he argues, slaves do not just sell their labor-power but are themselves commodities. Slaves also do not receive a wage, and, as such, they do not "generate internal demand" because they do not "form a consumer market." Nevertheless, Mintz maintained that different as the two forms of social relations may be, what makes New World slavery capitalist is that it was brought into being by the colonizing western European capitalist powers since the sixteenth century (Mintz 1978, 84, 91). Still, he went on,

> in spite of the citations from Marx, it is not completely clear, at least to me, just how he envisioned slavery—and particularly plantation slavery for the production of agricultural commodities for European markets—in his picture of world capitalism. I have suggested elsewhere that Marx himself may not have been wholly satisfied with his own understanding of how "slavery pure and simple" fit within capitalism—as when he refers to plantation owners in America as capitalists who "exist as anomalies within a world based on free labor." (Mintz 1978, 84–85)

In an earlier essay, Mintz had raised the same caveat when he wrote that

> Marx clearly recognized that, while it was analytically necessary to contrapose slavery and free labor in order to understand (and to dramatize) the emergence and consolidation of European capitalism, their "antagonism" did not mean they do not co-occur, or that there are no forms of labor-exaction which lie between them. (Mintz 1977, 259)

Robin Blackburn, on the other hand, argues that the plantation system of the New World was "constructed by and for the market, with the aim of maximizing commodity outputs so long as this yielded a surplus of revenues over costs." But he also noted that the plantations had characteristics of a "natural economy" and self-sufficiency insofar as the slaves produced some of their own food, made their own clothes, built the buildings of the plantations, and tended their masters and their families, all of which limited the planters' purchases. At the same time, the simple tools and implements the slaves used in the production process, as well as the slaves themselves, who were the most expensive items, had to be bought. Taxes and some salaries had to be paid (to hired agents, for example), so "the slave plantation had to justify its cash outlays by turning a profit" (Blackburn 2011, 67–68). "In short," he concluded, the plantation "was a hybrid type of enterprise, with modern features (looking forward to the industrial 'plant') but a basis in extra-economic compulsion"[3] (Blackburn 2011, 68).

Perhaps the theorist with the most unambiguous and consistent view of slavery as a capitalist social relation in the context of the capitalist world-economy is Immanuel Wallerstein. But it is also the case that Wallerstein, though influenced by Marx, is offering a different interpretation of that world-economy. He sees capitalism as a world-system[4] that since its emergence in the sixteenth century included forms of non-wage "labor control" (such as slavery or coerced cash-crop labor) in addition to those of wage-labor. For Wallerstein, three factors were necessary for the establishment of a capitalist world-economy: (1) the geographic expansion of the European world; (2) the development of different forms of labor control for different types of production in the different zones of the world-economy (i.e., an international division of labor); and (3) the establishment of relatively strong state machineries in the "core" states of this world-economy (Wallerstein 1974, 38). Thus, Wallerstein, extending and reformulating the argument of Andre Gunder Frank (1967), argues that capitalism emerged as the dominant social system in the sixteenth century and became the organizing principle of all other existing modes or forms of labor organization that survived "in function of how they fitted into a political-social framework deriving from capitalism" (Wallerstein 1974, 77). The expansion of the western European states and the establishment of colonies in the New World since the sixteenth century were the processes by which these areas became incorporated into the capitalist world-economy as "peripheral zones" to perform certain specific productive functions assigned to them by their position within the international division of labor.

Wallerstein's critique of what he called "ahistorical social science," including its Marxist variants, is based on what they take to be the unit of analysis. To understand the processes of social transformation over a long historical period, he argues, it's imperative to determine what the unit of analysis is in order to observe the structural changes that occurred over time. These time segments, however, are not "discrete but continuous in reality; *ergo* they are 'stages' in the 'development' of a social structure, a development which we determine however not *a priori* but *a posteriori*" (Wallerstein 1976, 3). It follows from this that the fundamental error of ahistorical Marxism is "to reify parts of the totality into such units and then to compare these reified structures" (Wallerstein 1976, 3).

Concretely, this means that by taking the nation-state rather than the totality of the world-system as a unit of analysis, "ahistorical Marxists" analyzing the "transition" from feudalism to capitalism have tried to determine which "mode of production" or form of remuneration of labor was dominant (in the sixteenth and seventeenth centuries) to determine whether a particular society or mode of production was "feudal" (i.e., where the laborer controlled the means of production and was allowed to keep part of the product for subsistence), "slave" (such as the plantation economies of the Caribbean in the sixteenth to nineteenth centuries), or "capitalist" (i.e., where the laborer turned over the whole product to the landowner/capitalist in return for a wage). For these theorists, Wallerstein argues, the fundamental issue "revolves around the existence of free labor as the defining characteristic of a capitalist mode of production. There in a nutshell it is. If proletarian, then capitalism. Of course. To be sure. But is England, or Mexico, or the West Indies, a unit of analysis? Does each have a separate 'mode of production'? Or is the unit (for the sixteenth–nineteenth centuries) the European world-economy, including England, and Mexico [and the West Indies], in which case what was the 'mode of production' of this world-economy?" (Wallerstein 1976, 9–10).[5]

The answer, for Wallerstein, was obvious. Since the sixteenth century this world-economy was capitalist, which he defined as a system of commodity "production for sale in a market in which the object is to realize the maximum profit. In such a system production is constantly expanded as long as further production is profitable, and men constantly innovate new ways of producing things that will expand the profit margin" (Wallerstein 1976, 15). By contrast, he argues, Marxists, including Marx himself, have confused this issue by focusing on the nation-state as the unit of analysis and arguing that the period from the sixteenth to the eighteenth centuries was one of a "transition" from feudalism to capitalism, which for him is "a blurry non-concept with no operational indicators" that leaves its proponents with the task of explaining why the "transition occurred at different rates and times in different countries" (Wallerstein 1976, 9–10). As I will show below, however, Wallerstein misread or misinterpreted Marx, who also considered the capitalist system to be global from its origin even if he may have seen England as the "classic" example because it is there that wage-labor relations developed most rapidly and allowed him to formulate his theory of surplus value. It does not follow, however, that Marx reduced the definition of capitalism to wage-labor, as others have done or as Wallerstein suggests.

For Wallerstein the confusion—of focusing on the nation-state as the unit of analysis—disappears if it can be shown that production of commodities for profit in a market was occurring during that period. Given that this was the case over a large geographical area that went from Poland in the northeast through western and southern Europe and much of the Western Hemisphere that formed a single division of labor to produce mostly agricultural products for sale and profit in the world market, it can simply be called a capitalist mode of production (Wallerstein 1976, 16). That mode of production, however, was not characterized by the prevalence of wage-labor, but comprised, in addition to wage-laborers, slaves, coerced cash-crop laborers, sharecropping, and tenancy as alternative forms of labor relations in the different geographic zones of the world-economy: the core, periphery, and semi-periphery that became stabilized circa 1640 (Wallerstein 1976, 16–18).

These three structural positions resulted from the development of strong states in northwest Europe and weaker ones in the peripheral areas. These unequal relations among stronger and weaker states led to the processes of "unequal exchange" among them. Thus,

> capitalism involves not only appropriation of the surplus value by an owner from a laborer, but an appropriation of surplus of the whole world-economy by core areas. And this was as true in the stage of agricultural capitalism as it is in the age of industrial capitalism. Capitalism was from the beginning an affair of the world-economy and not of nation-states. It is a misreading of the situation to claim that it is only in the twentieth century that capitalism has become "world-wide," although this claim is frequently made in various writings, particularly by Marxists. (Wallerstein 1976, 18–19)

From this it follows that the processes of unequal exchange, that is, the appropriation of surplus value by core areas from peripheral areas, also leads to their unequal development, and once this unequal structural relation is institutionalized it is impossible to overcome it in the short run. Part of the reason for this is the stabilizing role that semi-peripheral states perform as a "middle stratum" in the world-economy, thereby preventing the polarization of the world-system between core and periphery. "The existence of the third category means precisely that the upper stratum is not faced with the *unified* opposition of all the others because the *middle* stratum is both exploited and exploiter. It follows that the specific economic role is not all that important, and has thus changed throughout the various historical stages of the modern world-system" (Wallerstein 1976, 23, emphasis in original).

In his critique of Wallerstein, Robert Brenner called this view of capitalism as a world-economy that emerged in the sixteenth century comprising a single international division of labor that created the simultaneous processes of unequal exchange and unequal development through the appropriation of surplus value by the core areas from the semi-peripheral and peripheral areas "Neo-Smithian." In contrast, he advanced what he considered a more orthodox Marxist interpretation of the origin and development of capitalism in western Europe, England in particular, from the struggles between landlords and peasants that led to the emergence of free wage-labor, and not from the world market or world trade or European colonialism in the New World. As he put it, if Wallerstein argues that the pressures of the market "would lead to an evolution away from serfdom toward capitalism due to market-induced needs of the ruling class to increase production and thus to adopt new productive forces inoperable under the old [feudal] mode," then one cannot logically argue that "labor power as a commodity is *the* essential condition for economic development via accumulation and innovation. In that case, the dynamic of development clearly resides in trade, not in the class relations of labor power as a commodity" (Brenner 1977, 56, emphasis in original).

It follows from this, according to Brenner, that for Wallerstein capitalist development and underdevelopment are simultaneous processes resulting from the transfer of surpluses from the peripheral to the core areas. If that is the case, then it could not be that capitalist economic development resulted from the accumulation of capital through the innovation of the productive forces based on historically developed structures of class relations of free wage-labor. If, on the other hand, one starts from the position that class relations result from historically specific conflicts between classes "through which the direct producers have, to a greater or lesser extent, succeeded in restricting the form and extent of ruling-class access to surplus labour," then the way a given ruling class can or cannot maximize its surplus "may or may not at all correspond with the objective requirements for the development of the productive forces, i.e., output" (Brenner 1977, 60).

In that case, Brenner argues, ruling classes that have direct access to their means of subsistence and reproduction are not compelled to develop their productive forces because their survival and reproduction are not contingent on their ability to compete on the world market (Brenner 1977, 60). Thus, "neither economic development nor underdevelopment are *directly* dependent upon, caused by, one another. Each is the product of a specific evolution of class relations, *in part* determined historically '*outside*' capitalism, in relationship to non-capitalist modes" (Brenner 1977, 61, emphasis in original). For Brenner, then, Wallerstein cannot accept that viewpoint whereas for him capitalism does not develop/innovate the means of production via the accumulation of capital on the basis of free wage-labor, but rather from the view that such development in the core results from surpluses extracted from the peripheral areas, which in turn become underdeveloped because they lack capital (Brenner 1977, 61).

For Brenner, then, it is clear: economic development or underdevelopment, that is, the development of the productive forces or their stagnation, is caused not by a country's position in the division of labor of the world-economy or the transfer of surplus from the less developed to the more developed country, but foremost by the specific modes of surplus production and surplus extraction that are determined by that country's class or social relations of production (Brenner 1977, 66). He further critiques those Marxists who saw the "primitive accumulation of capital" resulting from "outright theft, from imperialism, from commercial profit, or even from the exploitation of labor for commercial profit" as capable of leading to the development of capitalism (Brenner 1977, 36). None of that, he insisted, would necessarily lead to the development of free wage-labor relations as the *conditio sine qua non* for capitalism. Put differently, the countries of western Europe, England in particular, where capitalism first developed were those whose systems of property ownership and their corresponding modes of surplus extraction compelled the emerging capitalist classes to develop their means of production and the productivity of their labor forces to increase the production of "relative" and not just "absolute" surplus value: "To account for capitalist economic development is, therefore, at least to explain the basis for this conjunction between the requirements for surplus extraction and the needs of the developing productive forces: on the one hand, its structure, or the reasons it held true; on the other hand, its origins, or how it came into being" (Brenner 1977, 68).

This does not mean, however, that the world market played no role in Brenner's argument on the origin and development of capitalism in western Europe. But for him, it was the transformations within the class structure and the system of production, especially in English agriculture in the seventeenth century, that made the market significant. The key factor was the growth in what he called the three-tiered relations of landlord, capitalist tenant, and free wage-labor—that is, the separation of the immediate producer from the means of production—that made possible the accumulation of capital by improving the productive forces in agriculture (Brenner 1977, 75). To survive, the tenants who leased their lands from the landlords and hence had to pay rents to the latter were compelled to specialize and increase agricultural outputs by improving the methods of production in order to sell their products at market prices and make a profit. Similarly, it served the landlords' interests to invest in their farms' infrastructure and benefit from their tenants' profits as well (Brenner 1977, 76).

At this juncture the world market became significant. The increasing demand in Europe for English cloth manufactures from the late fifteenth century onward created more demand for English agricultural products, which, in turn, provided the incentives to English landlords and their tenants to consolidate and improve their lands and means of production in order to extract more surplus/profit from their hired workers created by the abolition of serfdom and peasant property (Brenner 1977, 77). Thus, in contrast to other parts of Europe where exports in manufactured goods declined during the seventeenth century, the increasing demand for agricultural, manufactured, and consumer goods in England led not only to the growth of the home market but to the development of the English economy as a whole. For Brenner, then, the origin of capitalist development in England is to be explained by the specific historical conditions and processes that had led to the abolition of serfdom and the undermining of peasant property, on the one hand, and the consequent rise in free labor and the improvement of the means of production to increase profits and capital accumulation, on the other. "Clearly, this two-sided development is inexplicable as the result of ruling-class policy or ruling-class intention, but was the outcome of processes of class formation, rooted in class conflict" (Brenner 1977, 78).

As Wallerstein had previously suggested, Alexander Anievas and Kerem Nisancioglu also criticized Brenner for his reductionist argument, which takes the concept of "social property relations," in his case the wage-labor relations, as the singular form of labor exploitation that defines the capitalist mode of production. "The result of this ontological singularity," they argue, is "a dual tunneling—both temporal and spatial—of our empirical field of inquiry" (Anievas and Nisancioglu 2015, 24). As such, the origin of capitalism is reduced to the "manifestation of one conceptual moment—the freeing of labour—and in turn explained by it," which is then used to limit the rise of capitalism to "a single geographic region—the English countryside—immune from wider intersocietal developments" (Anievas and Nisancioglu 2015, 24).

As with Brenner, Ellen Meiksins Wood, in *The Origin of Capitalism: A Longer View* (2002), critiqued the "commercialization model" that assumed that the capitalist market is "an opportunity rather than an imperative," and that capitalism will arise once the "obstacles and fetters" of the old feudal relations are removed (Wood 2002, 42). Wood also focused on Brenner's insistence on looking for the factors that created the compulsion or imperative for the landlords, tenants, and laborers to depend on the market for their survival—profits for the lord and tenant, wages for the laborers—by improving agricultural "productivity by means of innovative land use and techniques not to mention the increasing exploitation of wage labor" (Wood 2002, 54). In other words, for Wood, as it was for Brenner, the specificity of capitalism emerges when the immediate producers become dependent on the market and the imperatives of competition to access their means of production, even when they may not yet be entirely separated from them (Wood 2002, 61). As she put it, the key difference between all previous systems of production and capitalism is not whether production occurs in urban or rural areas, but has everything to do with the specific property relations between producers and appropriators: "Only in capitalism is the dominant mode of appropriation based on the complete dispossession of the direct producers, who (unlike chattel slaves) are legally free and whose surplus labor is appropriated by purely 'economic' means [and] without direct coercion" (Wood 2002, 96). And for her, as it was for Brenner, it was in England that this new system of property relations and its market-driven compulsions emerged in the sixteenth century, first in agriculture before spreading to other sectors and branches of production (Wood 2002, 100–103). Market compulsion and its imperatives, then, become the decisive and distinctive characteristics of capitalism, and compel capitalists and all other economic actors, workers, and other producers, to constantly improve the methods and techniques of production, constantly accumulate by searching for new markets, and impose its imperatives on new territories and all aspects and spheres of human life (Wood 2002, 97; 2003, 9).

But, perhaps aware of the reductionist and Eurocentric nature of this argument, she, unlike Brenner, sought to take other factors into account that may have contributed to the origin and development of capitalism. In this context, in *Empire of Capital* (2003), Wood focused on contrasting the market systems that operated in other societies before the rise of capitalism in England in the sixteenth century and the new transformative dynamics they unleashed to impose their logic and imperatives on all others. For my purpose here, however, I will focus on the two most important "Empires of Commerce" she analyzed—the Venetian and the Dutch—to contrast them with what she thought was fundamentally different about the "Empire of Capital" England created since the sixteenth century.[6] Both of those commercial empires were engaged in extensive commodity trades produced primarily in their urban cities, such as textile, silk, and glass in Venice, and agricultural goods for the urban markets in Holland.

In the case of Venice, urban merchants invested in the production of commodities in response to market opportunities, but trade and financial services were greater sources of wealth. Rather than being driven by price competition, trade was based largely on monopoly privileges aided by advanced commercial and financial practices and by the imposition of colonial military force on Crete and Cyprus where they used slaves for sugar production. The Venetians did not themselves exploit the slaves on those plantations but benefited mostly by supplying the slaves to those colonies. Thus, even though market competition led to changes in and improvement of the production of domestic goods, they remained dependent on their "extra-economic" advantages in controlling markets and the trades in both domestic and imported goods: "Political power in the city was at the same time economic power; and in external trade, which was by far the most lucrative commercial activity, military force remained the basic condition of commercial success" (Wood 2003, 57).

The Dutch Republic, however, was a very different case. It was the most commercialized state in Europe at the time due to its vast commercial empire that stretched from the Baltic to the East Indies, Africa, and the Americas as the early leaders in the transatlantic slave trade. As with the Venetians, it was also less directly involved in the exploitation of slaves in colonial plantations. Given the enormous significance of trade for the Dutch Republic, most of the population became trade dependent, including farmers and especially the urban population tied to the global commercial and financial enterprise (Wood 2003, 63).

Trade dependence, however, meant that the cities did not rely exclusively on Dutch agricultural production to meet their food and other needs. But urban growth nonetheless raised overall demand, and this in turn fostered capital investments and improvements in agricultural production and labor productivity to help meet that demand. Dutch producers and farmers, in other words, seemed to be responding to market imperatives and compulsion, which, according to Wood, is the definition of capitalism. But she insisted that it was not, because "the Dutch Republic in many ways still operated on familiar non-capitalist principles, above all in its dependence on extra-economic powers of appropriation" (Wood 2003, 63). Dutch merchants remained "at one remove" from domestic production and relied instead on commercial sophistication more than competitive production: "Their vocation was, to put it simply, circulation, not production, and profit was generated by that means" (Wood 2003, 63).

England, by contrast, would create a capitalist empire driven by the economic imperatives associated with that system, as she proposed above. But creating the property relations associated with capitalism domestically, even if they required some use of force, is not the same as doing so abroad, where brute force was absolutely necessary, hence the need to conquer and colonize other territories. Unlike the previous commercial empires that established colonies to profit from their trade, English imperialism was driven by the "capitalist imperatives emanating from the imperial homeland" and not the other way around. Whatever historians may argue "about the contribution of empire to the development of British capitalism, it seems indisputable that the development of capitalism at home in Britain determined the shape of British capitalism" (Wood 2003, 89).

British imperialism, in other words, was not just about acquiring colonies for trade advantages and commercial supremacy; it was primarily about establishing capitalist principles for the purpose of accumulating capital from the production of surplus value through competitive production for the market (Wood 2003, 100). Even if, Wood argues, the justification for such an imperialism drew from noncommercial, extra-economic ideologies of racial or cultural inferiority to justify it, "they were deeply affected by capitalism's reliance on economic imperatives" (Wood 2003, 89).[7] In other words, given that capitalist exploitation is a market relation, it necessitates a conceptual framework that stresses a contractual relation between "legally free and equal individuals," which "made capitalism compatible with ideologies of civic freedom and equality in a way that non-capitalist class systems never were" (Wood 2003, 101).[8] We are thus back to the reductionist search for the singular "social property relations" of free wage-labor to explain capitalism's origin. Orlando Patterson offered a succinct response to such claims. Given that capitalism has been equated with free wage-labor, slavery challenged that reduction at the same time that it exposed the reality behind so-called free labor: "The problem that slavery created for the U.S. South and other capitalistic slave systems, therefore, was not economic but ideological" (Patterson 1982, 33).

A problem arose in the English colonies of the Americas, however. There, the unavailability of "free and equal" individuals in most of those colonies required slavery, which then necessitated the deployment of a racist ideology to justify it given that the slaves in question were Africans. Even if initially British colonialists imported indentured servants from England, they proved insufficient to supply the growing demand for labor on the tobacco, sugar, and cotton plantations, so slavery became the alternative. Just as the Dutch and Venetians had done before, the English and their other European rivals (the Spanish, the Portuguese, and the French especially) also relied on African slaves as the principal labor force in their American colonies (Wood 2003, 105).

Wood clearly acknowledged, then, that capitalism has "at certain points in its development, appropriated to itself, and even intensified, non-capitalist modes of exploitation" such as slavery. British capitalism, then, not only gave an impetus to "this old form of exploitation" and even boosted the demand for it in the colonies "at a time when capitalist social property relations made other forms of dependent labor unavailable and a mass of free proletarians did not yet exist" (Wood 2003, 105). It is therefore "impossible to deny" that slavery played an "essential part in producing its highly profitable commodities, tobacco and sugar. Nor can it be denied that industrialization at home, based as it was on the production of cotton textiles, would depend on colonial cotton produced by slaves in the West Indies" (Wood 2003, 105).

If that is the case, then, this must mean that capitalism cannot be reduced to free wage-labor as the *conditio sine qua non* for its property and social relations of production and the exclusion of all others, as she and Brenner insisted. It is clear from her own account that the slaves in the American colonies, just as the free wage-laborers in England, were producing surplus value, that is, capital in Marx's meaning of the word, and that the plantations were driven by the imperatives and logic of the market. Expressed differently, capitalism as a global system incorporated areas in its sphere of production that were based on slave property relations to produce commodities— and hence surplus value—for sale in a market and were compelled to do so by market imperatives.

By conceding that capitalism relied (and continues to rely) on other forms of labor relations to create surplus value and the accumulation of capital,

Wood in effect conceded Wallerstein's argument. If, as she claimed, it was the "capitalist imperatives emanating from the imperial homeland," that propelled England to create slave plantation economies in the Americas, what imperatives propelled the Spanish, the Portuguese, and the French to do the same when they were not using those colonies only for trade advantages—which they certainly were—but were directly involved in the exploitation of their slave labor forces to accumulate capital as England was? Clearly, they could not have been feudal economies because according to her, only capitalism imposes market compulsion on its actors to accumulate capital through the direct appropriation of surplus labor from the production of commodities by the direct producers, in this case the slaves on the plantation economies of the Americas.

TOWARD AN ALTERNATIVE PERSPECTIVE

In the introduction to *Grundrisse: Foundations of the Critique of Political Economy* (Marx 1973), Marx spelled out his methodology for the analysis of the capitalist mode of production, which he always conceived of as a global social system since its origins in the sixteenth century. As he expressed it: "When we consider a given country politico-economically, we begin with its population, its distribution among classes, town, country, the coast, the different branches of production, export and import, annual production and consumption, commodity prices, etc." (Marx 1973, 100). While this may seem to be the right way to begin an investigation with the concrete and existing preconditions, this proves not to be the case, for the following reasons:

> The population is an abstraction if I leave out, for example, the classes of which it is composed. These classes in turn are an empty phrase if I am not familiar with the elements on which they rest, e.g. wage labour, capital, etc. These latter in turn presuppose exchange, division of labour, prices, etc. For example, capital is nothing without wage labour, without value, money, price, etc. Thus, if I were to begin with the population, this would be a chaotic conception of the whole, and I would then, by means of further determination, move analytically towards ever more simple concepts, from the imagined concrete towards ever thinner abstractions until I had arrived at the simplest determinations. From there the journey would have to be retraced until I had finally arrived at the population again, but this time not as the chaotic conception of a whole, but as a rich totality of many determinations and relations.

> The concrete is concrete because it is the concentration of many determi-
> nations, hence unity of the diverse. It appears in the process of thinking,
> therefore, as a process of concentration, as a result, not as a point of departure,
> even though it is the point of departure in reality and hence also the point of
> departure for observation and conception. Along the first path the full concep-
> tion was evaporated to yield an abstract determination; along the second, the
> abstract determinations lead towards a reproduction of the concrete by way of
> thought. (Marx 1973, 100–101)

The significance of this long passage is twofold. First, Marx is making a distinction between the abstract concepts and categories that define and are specific to the capitalist mode of production and the actual, concrete development of that social system in time and space. Second, identifying the concepts that define and are specific to a mode of production as a necessary starting point to reconstruct its actual, concrete historical development is not the same as reducing that mode of production to its essential core elements, in this case, the existence of free wage-labor (Hall 1974, 147). As Marx explained it, insofar as capitalism is the most complex historical system of production, the "categories which express its relations, the comprehension of its structure, thereby also allows insights into the structure and the relations of production of all the vanished social formations out of whose ruins and elements it built itself up, whose partly still unconquered remnants are carried along within it, whose nuances have developed explicit significance within it, etc." (Marx 1973, 105). In short, the abstract concepts that define a mode of social production have to be able to account for or explain the concrete, real relations that constitute it.

As Stuart Hall pointed out, when analyzing any historical phenomenon or relation it is necessary to understand its internal structure and what distinguishes it as well as those other structures to which it is combined and forms an inclusive totality:

> Both the specificities and the connections—the complex unities of struc-
> tures—have to be demonstrated by the concrete analysis of concrete relations
> and conjunctions. If relations are mutually articulated, but remain specified by
> their difference, this articulation, and the determinate conditions on which it
> rests, has to be demonstrated. The method thus retains concrete empirical
> reference as a privileged and undissolved "moment" within a theoretical analy-
> sis without thereby making it "empiricist": the concrete analysis of concrete
> situations. (Hall 1974, 147)

In other words, capital may be nothing without wage-labor, as Marx said, because based on wage-labor he arrived at the concept of necessary and surplus labor time, of surplus value (absolute and relative),[9] and profit. It constitutes the dominant production relation of that mode of production, and hence serves as the point of departure for its abstract conceptualization. But this abstract conceptualization must not be confused with the actual, concrete characteristics and manifestations/operations of that mode of production in space and time, which are the product of many determinations that include, among other factors, the use of labor relations and exploitation other than wage-labor, such as slavery, for example.

Dale Tomich suggested also that distinguishing Marx's method of abstraction from historical accounts of capitalist development allows us to "reincorporate in the field of analysis those 'historical contingencies and accidents' that were eliminated in the process of abstraction" (Tomich 2004, 28). This more "open analytical framework" allows us to "focus on particular relations as themselves outcomes of complex historical processes," which makes it possible to consider "slavery and other forms of unwaged labor into the totality of political economic relations. This approach does not treat wage labor and slave labor as external to one another, nor does it eliminate the differences between them and assimilate both into a homogeneous conception of capital" (Tomich 2004, 30). Thus, considering the "unity and heterogeneity of the historical field in which these relations operate and from which they derive their meaning," makes it possible to avoid treating these social relations as "ideal-typical conceptions" that are "practically independent of one another" (Tomich 2004, 76).

Anievas and Nisancioglu expressed the same point in a different way. Although free wage-labor is certainly integral and central to the definition of capitalism, it is neither necessary nor useful to "claim that [it] can only exist where the majority of the direct producers are 'free'" (Anievas and Nisancioglu 2015, 31). In short, if "history is a messy, complex affair, full of accidents, contingencies and the untheorizable [p]roblems emerge when the central objects of our theories . . . are considered pure contingencies in relation to the abstractions we seek to explain them with" (Anievas and Nisancioglu 2015, 32). These, I believe, were the central errors of Brenner's and Wood's reductionist approach to the study of capitalism.

"The circulation of money is the starting point of capital," Marx argues, and the "production of commodities and their circulation in its developed form, namely trade, form the historic presupposition under which capital arises. World trade and the world market date from the sixteenth century, and from then on the modern history of capital starts to unfold" (Marx 1976, 247). From the outset, then, Marx understood that capitalism was a global system that compelled the nation-states that comprised it at any particular point in time to conform to its modus operandi:

> The discovery of gold and silver in America, the extirpation, enslavement and entombment in mines of the indigenous population of that continent, the beginnings of the conquest and plunder of India, and the conversion of Africa into a preserve for the commercial hunting of blackskins [*sic*], are all things which characterize the dawn of the era of capitalist production. (Marx 1976, 915)

He goes on to say that the colonies established by Spain, Portugal, Holland, France, and England, "in more or less chronological order [employed] the power of the state, the concentrated and organized force of society, to hasten, as in a hothouse, the process of transformation of the feudal mode of production into the capitalist mode, and to shorten the transition. Force is the midwife of every old society which is pregnant with a new one. It is itself an economic power" (Marx 1976, 915–16).

The relations established among expansionist western Europe since the sixteenth century, the New World, Africa, and the Orient, laid the foundations for the creation of a world economic system dominated by western Europe. The system of international trade established by the western European powers made possible the accumulation of capital that partly fueled the industrial development of the eighteenth and nineteenth centuries. The conquest of the Americas had the immediate effect of dumping precious metals on the European market. The supply of gold and silver became particularly abundant after the conquest of Mexico in 1522 and Peru in 1535, the discovery of the silver mines of Potosi in Upper Peru in 1545, and the application of mercury to extract the mineral around 1554 (Mousnier 1965, 4:89).

The need for new supplies of food and fuel was another reason for overseas expansion and trade with the Mediterranean and Atlantic islands, north and west Africa, eastern Europe, the Russian steppes, and central Asia (Wallerstein 1974, 42). The Mediterranean specialized in grain exports, particularly wheat, barley, and millet. Salt, salt fish, and food preserved in salt were also items of trade, as well as wine, cheese, and cooking oil (Parry 1967, 4:155–60). Sugar had become an important complement in the European diet, as a source of calories, as a substitute for fats, and as a source of alcoholic beverages, particularly rum. From its Mediterranean origins, sugar followed European expansion into the Americas (Wallerstein 1974, 43; Mintz 1985, passim). From India, Ceylon, and Indonesia came the much sought-after spices, which, after the crisis that beset the Mediterranean trade, opened the way for a direct Portuguese trade with India by way of the Cape of Good Hope. The Portuguese became the principal suppliers of spices to western Europe, displacing the Venetians (Parry 1967, 4:163–64).

The need for clothing was yet another reason for expansion. In addition to the extant luxury silk trade, the growing textile industries required raw materials such as dye-stuffs used for dyeing cotton and woolen cloths and gum used to stiffen silk goods (Wallerstein 1974, 45). However, European trade was not confined to importing raw materials, foods, and woods, or to exporting manufactured goods. The trade also included crops and livestock and influenced developments in western Europe and the overseas territories with which they traded. There is no doubt that the period of the great discoveries and European colonial expansion were highly significant for the western European economies. This period (from the sixteenth century to the Industrial Revolution of the eighteenth and nineteenth centuries), was the height of the influence of mercantile capitalism, or state-regulated trade for the benefit of the European powers engaged in it.

In short, as Kenneth Pomeranz pointed out, the western European colonial and global expansion since the sixteenth century made it possible for it to overcome some of its disadvantages in agriculture and land management, the inefficient use of certain land-intensive products such as fuel wood, and land-saving technologies. Western Europe's global expansion and colonialism allowed it to obtain land-intensive resources and reduce its ecological strain "without having to reallocate vast amounts of their own labor to the various labor-intensive activities that would have been necessary to manage their own land for higher yield and greater ecological sustainability." The "external factors," in other words, made it possible for Europe's technological inventions to have a more "revolutionary impact on the economy and society than the marginal technological improvements that continued to occur in eighteenth-century China, India, and elsewhere" (Pomeranz 2000, 32).

It does not follow, however, that all the European countries that established colonies in the New World, plundered the resources and enslaved and murdered the populations of the conquered territories, and transferred their accumulated wealth to the mother country would develop their domestic economies and manufacturing production at the same rate. Nevertheless, once these countries developed their industrial capacities and increased the production of commodities and capital accumulation domestically by transforming the old feudal relations into wage-labor relations, they also sought to expand the world market into new territories, regions, and countries to exploit them on an ever-larger scale. As Marx put it, if "[today], industrial supremacy brings with it commercial supremacy, [in] the period of manufacture it is the reverse: commercial supremacy produces industrial predominance. Hence the preponderance played by the colonial system at that time" (Marx 1976, 918).

But it was not only in the era of early colonialism and New World slavery (sixteenth to nineteenth centuries) that capitalism gave rise to an international division of labor and the exploitation of the labor (domestic or imported) and resources of the colonized territories for the benefit of the colonizing powers. Their industrialization would compel them to search for new markets, new sources of raw materials and production, and the demand for more workers to exploit, while they discarded their own workers as a result of technological innovation:

> By constantly turning workers into "supernumeraries," large-scale industry, in all countries where it has taken root, spurs on rapid increases in emigration and the colonization of foreign lands, which are thereby converted into settlements for growing the raw material for the mother country. By ruining handicraft production of finished articles in other countries, machinery converts them into fields for the production of raw materials. Thus India was compelled to produce cotton, hemp, jute and indigo for Great Britain. A new and international division of labor springs up, one suited to the requirements of the main industrial countries, and it converts one part of the globe into a chiefly agricultural field of production for supplying the other part, which remains a preeminently industrial field. (Marx 1976, 579–80)

It is clear, then, that for Marx capitalism was from its beginnings in the sixteenth century a global or world system that relied on the strength of the states of western Europe to create an international division of labor to exploit the human and natural resources of the peoples, countries, and territories they colonized and dominated to produce commodities for the world market and accumulate capital for their benefit. It is also clear that what Marx has been describing here are the processes of uneven geographical and regional development associated with the rise of global capitalism since the sixteenth century. To be sure, the specific class relations in the different countries that became integrated in this new capitalist world economy and division of labor would play a significant role in either fostering or impeding the development of the productive forces and hence their industrialization. And this is where, among others, the key differences between wage-labor relations and slavery are to be found (such as at the ideological level: rights and freedom versus slavery and unfreedom), as I will explain below. But there is also no doubt that the transfer of the wealth produced or plundered in the dominated and colonized territories would be a factor in those processes of uneven development.

Given that to be the case, then, Marx's argument differs from both Brenner's and Wallerstein's respective formulations discussed above. For Marx, unlike Brenner, there is a double process of exploitation and surplus transfer from less developed to more developed economies resulting from the exploitation of both their resources and their workers, whether they be wage-laborers, slaves, tenant farmers, day laborers, or *corvée* laborers. But he also understood that if the countries that have been transformed into producers of commodities for export to the imperial centers developed their economies by proletarianizing their laboring classes, they, too, could make the transition from the production of absolute to relative surplus value and the concomitant development of their forces of production. For Wallerstein, on the other hand, the relations between core and peripheral countries are determinant, and not the specific class relations that facilitate or inhibit development in the latter because they lack the capital to do so, as Brenner pointed out. Put differently, the issue here is not the appropriation of a surplus by an owner from a worker, as Wallerstein phrased it. It has to do, rather, with the effects that specific social relations of production have in facilitating or hindering the development of the productive forces.

Here, I think, David Harvey offered an important clarification. As he explained it, the constant search by the European-centered capitalist system for new territories to produce and accumulate capital became incorporated through what he called "accumulation through dispossession" (Harvey 2006, 92). Areas that possess abundant natural resources, be they agricultural, mineral, or other endowments, can be transformed into spaces of production and specialization. Similarly, the competitive requirements of capitalist accumulation compel capitalists to relocate production to more advantageous locations or regions, processes that then produce or exacerbate uneven geographic development, such that over time some regions become richer while others become poorer (Harvey 2006, 98). These processes and structures of uneven geographical/regional development, however, are always negotiated and contingent on the particular class configurations and social relations of production, the forms of governance and relative strengths of the ruling classes and alliances they form with other national class factions or those of other states, the results of which either facilitate or impede national development (Harvey 2006, 103).

Similarly, resource-abundant regions can become depleted or abandoned for cheaper alternatives produced elsewhere, just as technological changes can render previous infrastructures and capacities irrelevant. Thus, class and other social or cultural struggles as well as changes in the requirements and shifting patterns of capital accumulation can and do affect regional structures. Regionality, in other words, is "always 'under production' as well as 'in the course of modification' through capital accumulation. Further capital accumulation always has to negotiate, confront, and if necessary revolutionize the regional structures that it had earlier produced. Capitalism cannot exist without engagements of this sort" (Harvey 2006, 104).

CAPITALISM AND SLAVERY IN SAINT-DOMINGUE

In the specific case that concerns me here, namely the French colony of Saint-Domingue from the seventeenth century to the end of the eighteenth, and Haiti since then, the creation of this zone of production initially based on slavery was part of what Sven Beckert referred to as the "beating heart of this new system" that required the capture and transportation of millions of Africans to the Americas, which in turn made India a more important source of cotton cloth production as well as a greater European mercantile presence in Africa. It was that global network of trade and production that gave enormous economic significance to the "territories captured in the Americas, and thus to overcome Europe's own resource constraints" (Beckert 2014, 37).

France had been planning to establish colonies in the New World since the sixteenth century. [10] But it was not until the mid-seventeenth century that it was able to challenge Spanish dominance and conquer territories in the Caribbean along with Britain and Holland. It was also Spain that introduced both sugar production and slavery in the first major island it colonized, namely the Arawakan-speaking Taino nation of Ayiti, which it renamed Española or Hispaniola in 1492. Following what Franklin Knight referred to as a systematic "campaign of barbarity" by the Spanish (Knight 1978, 25), combined with the diseases they brought with them (smallpox, measles, typhoid fever, the common cold) and against which the Tainos had no immunity, the population, estimated at more than 1 million in 1492, had been reduced to 60,000 by 1507 (Madiou 1989, 1:16; Nau 1894, 259).[11] Unable to entice more workers to emigrate from Spain (including convicts, among others), the colonial settlers turned to enslaving Lucayans (the Bahamas and Turks and Caicos islands today) and Caribs from the Lesser Antilles before they turned exclusively to Africa to obtain their slave laborers. With more Spanish settlers emigrating to South America and Mexico in search of quicker fortunes, the western third of the island had become virtually abandoned, making it easier for France to make its move and secure control of it with the Treaty of Riswick in 1697, and rename it *La partie française de l'le de Saint-Domingue* (Cabon 1929, 1:7; Dorsinville 1961, 6; Madiou 1988, 1:17–20).

My objective here is not to retrace the history of the development of Saint-Domingue except to say that, thanks to its constant replenishing of its slave population with new imports and its fertile soil, it went on to become the most productive and wealthiest Caribbean colony in the eighteenth century. Seventy-two percent of the slaves France transported from Africa went to Saint-Domingue by the mid-eighteenth century, and 90 percent by 1789. The 455,000 slaves it possessed in 1789 were more than those of Jamaica, Guadeloupe, and Martinique combined; and its 793 sugar plantations, 3,117 coffee plantations, 3,150 indigo plantations, and 789 cotton plantations outproduced all the other French and English colonies put together. By 1789 Saint-Domingue was exporting an annual average of 140 million pounds of sugar valued at 115 million *livres*, and an annual average of 250 million *livres* for all the goods exported to France, transported there by some 1,400 ships (see Dupuy 1989, 20–21).

But Saint-Domingue did not produce wealth only for the benefit of the French merchant bourgeoisie and its French and Creole planter classes.[12] It was also enormously beneficial to the French port cities involved in the colonial and slave trades—Bordeaux, Nantes, La Rochelle, Marseilles, Rouen, Orleans, Dieppe, Lille, Dunkerque—and the manufactures that refined the sugar, built the ships, and produced iron, rope, textiles and cloths, chemicals, flour, cooking oil, salted beef, prunes, and wines. C. L. R. James also offered this summary:

> In 1789 exchanges with the American colonies were 296 millions. France exported to the islands 78 millions of flour, salted meats, wines and stuffs. The colonies sent to France 218 millions of sugar, coffee, cocoa, wood, indigo, and hides. Of the 218 millions imported only 71 millions were consumed in France. The rest was exported after preparation. The total value of the colonies

represented 3,000 millions, and on them depended the livelihood of a number of Frenchmen variously estimated at between two and six millions. By 1789 San Doming was the market of the new world. (James 1963, 49–50)

In my view, then, it is clear that Saint-Domingue and the other French Caribbean colonies were fully integrated in the capitalist world market dominated by merchant capital and interacted with the other Western powers through the mediation of the French commercial bourgeoisie. The predominantly agricultural commodities produced by the slaves were coordinated and integrated with the manufactured and agricultural goods produced in France and exported to other western European economies and beyond. All of them contributed to the accumulation of capital and the development of the productive forces there but limited them in Saint-Domingue (Dupuy 1989, 22–23).

Marx also put it succinctly:

The indirect slavery of the proletariat [in Europe], the direct slavery of the Blacks in Surinam, in Brazil, in the southern regions of North America . . . is as much the pivot upon which our present-day industrialization turns as are machinery, credit, etc. Without slavery there could be no cotton, without cotton there could be no modern industry. It is slavery which has given value to the colonies, it is the colonies which have created world trade, and world trade is the necessary condition for large-scale machine industry. Consequently prior to the slave trade, the colonies sent very few products to the Old World and did not noticeably change the face of the world. Slavery, therefore, is an economic category of paramount importance. Being an economic category, slavery has existed in all nations since the beginning of the world. All that modern nations have achieved is to disguise slavery at home and import it openly into the New World. (Marx 1976, 167)

Given that to be the case, then, there is no way to characterize the slave-based economies and the slave relations of production in the New World other than that they were capitalist, and not just in the "broad sense" of the term as I wrote before,[13] because they did not exist autonomously but were fully embedded in the capitalist system created by the metropolitan powers. In his recent case study of a slave plantation in the fertile and very productive Cul de Sac plain of Saint-Domingue, Paul Cheney has shown how the plantation system was created for and functioned according to market imperatives, at the same time that it also sought to encourage self-sufficiency by allowing the slaves to cultivate the provision grounds provided to them (Cheney 2017,

42–43). On the plantation, "slaves were treated as units of capital to be purchased, set to work, maintained, and occasionally sold, all according to rational managerial principles," notwithstanding the fact that the masters also had to provide for their needs. But it was also clear that these two aspects of a typical plantation clashed in such a way that "the incessant demands for profitability that threatened slaves' lives and well-being" were countered by "considerations of interest [that] could temper the violence inherent in the despotic relation of master and slave" (Cheney 2017, 71).

Robin Blackburn, as had Mintz, pointed out that one of the key differences between a slave and a wage-laborer was that the planter had to buy and pay for his/her slave (whether outright or on credit), as well as the provisions for the slave, in advance of his/her labor in anticipation of future profits. By contrast, the capitalist employer paid the wage-laborer after he/she had possession of the product, even if there was a lag time before the product was sold (Blackburn 2011, 336). Yet, while it is true that slaves were part of the "fixed," or "constant," as opposed to the "variable" capital investment of the plantations, planters used their slaves in many different ways, such as selling them when necessary, using them as collateral to obtain loans or credit, or, on occasion, renting them to other planters when they needed additional workers. As such, then, as Trevor Burnard and John Garrigus put it, "slaves represented highly liquid forms of capital, as well as being people who produced income for their owners. Despite this 'fixed-cost' labor situation, sugar planters' attitude that their enslaved workers were flexible and expendable capital investments was consistent with an emerging industrial mentality" (Burnard and Garrigus 2016, 7–8).

But another important difference, I would argue, has to do with the question of technological innovation in a slave-based economy versus one based on wage-labor to increase the productivity of labor and thus reduce the number of slaves to be bought, as happens when machinery displaces wage-laborers. In his study of two plantations in Saint-Domingue, Gabriel Debien showed that even if the owners did not always keep elaborate and separate accounts of the total capital invested, the value added to that capital, the expenditures for the purchase of slaves and equipment, or the goods produced, the planters could calculate the profitability of their plantations accurately. The records of one of those plantations, for example, showed that it yielded an annual average rate of profit of 15 percent (Debien 1945, 1:10–12). Similarly, Hilliard d'Auberteuil calculated that a plantation with a total investment of 1,810,000 *livres*, 300 *carreaux*—about 960 acres—for cultivation, a water mill and refinery, slave quarters and other buildings worth 300,000 *livres*; the master's quarters for 20,000; tools and carts at 30,000; 500 slaves worth 900,000; and 50,000 for livestock, could regain its initial investment in eight years of peace, and this by only putting two-thirds of the land under cultivation: 150 *carreaux* for the cultivation of sugarcane, and 50 for the slaves' provision grounds, gardens, and living quarters (Hilliard d'Auberteuil 1776, 1:235).

The issue, then, is not the profitability of slave labor. The question, rather, is whether the plantation owners (or their hired managers) could increase the productivity of their slaves by means of technological innovation (i.e., increasing the productivity of the slaves by mechanizing the production process). As Marx argues in the case of the wage-laborer, when machines are employed in the production process to decrease the number of workers needed *and* increase the productivity and profitability of those employed— that is, the production of relative surplus value—they also reduce the value of the labor-power of the workers and increase the competition among them, such that there is a direct relationship between machinery and the "number of workers whose conditions of existence have been destroyed" by them (Marx 1976, 447).

Such is not the case in a slave-based economy, however. Insofar as the slave was both *constant* and *variable* capital, that is, a part of the capital invested by the master *and* labor-power, to displace him/her with machinery as could be done with the wage-laborer would amount to a net loss for the master who already bought the slave in advance of putting him/her to work. Such practices could undermine the basis for slavery itself if introduced on a large scale in *all* aspects of the production process (cutting, harvesting, transporting, milling, and refining the juice extracted from the sugarcanes). That is why as long as slavery relied on the extensive use of the slave—that is, the production of absolute surplus value—and the supply of new slaves could be secured, the incentive for the master was to literally work the slave to death to extract the maximum surplus labor from him/her and buy more slaves. That is exactly what happened. As Gwendolyn Hall pointed out, in Saint-Domingue the "masters calculated that the work of a *négresse* during an eight-month period (that is, the last three months of pregnancy and the months during which she breast-fed her infant) was worth 600 *livres*, and that during this time she was able to do only half of her normal work. The master therefore lost 300 *livres*. A fifteen-month-old slave was not worth this sum" (Hall 1971, 24; also cited in Neptune Anglade 1986, 94). On the basis of such

strictly inhumane business calculations, plantation owners in Saint-Domingue opted instead to renew their slave population every ten years on
average (Debien 1962; Léon 1963).[14]

However, all this does not mean that there was *no* technological innovation under slavery. Rather, such innovation was limited—in the eighteenth
century—to experimenting with new irrigation systems and new methods of
milling and refining the juice extracted from the cane to increase output, and
where the number of slaves needed was smaller in comparison to those
employed in the fields to plant, cut, and harvest the canes (Cheney 2017,
65–68; Burnard and Garrigus 2016, 247–48). But there is no question that
until the uprising of the slaves of Saint-Domingue in 1791 that destroyed its
sugar industry, the buying of more and more slaves and exploiting them to
death remained the primary basis of the colony's productivity and its immense wealth. The new rulers of Saint-Domingue (1800–1803) and Haiti
after 1804 tried to revive the plantation system by transforming the former
slaves into wage-laborers who would receive up to one-quarter of the value
of the crops and allowed to cultivate their own provision grounds. But they
resisted their proletarianization fiercely and fought instead to become subsistence farmers on their own land.

In addition to Jamaica, which remained as the most productive English
colony in the eighteenth century, sugar production moved to Puerto Rico, the
Dominican Republic, Cuba, and Barbados in the nineteenth century. A brief
consideration of the case of Cuba will suffice to illustrate my argument about
the limits of technological innovation in a slave-based economy—that is, the
use of labor-saving/displacing technology—because it became the world's
largest sugar producer between 1829 and 1883. Slavery was abolished there
in 1881 (Moreno Fraginals 1985, 15).

Between the 1820s and 1860s, many labor-saving and capital-intensive
technological improvements were introduced in the mills, such as the use of
steam power that replaced the previous animal- or water-powered grinding
mills, the vacuum pan, and the centrifuge to extract the cane's juice for
refining (Tomich 2004, 82; Moreno Fraginals 1976, 82–85). Animal-pow-
ered rail carriers were used, and between 1837 and 1851 steam-powered
trains were also used on the larger estates and eventually in all sugar-growing
areas to carry the sugar to the ports. These technological advances also led to
land concentrations and the creation of larger estates at the expense of smaller ones, and to a demand for more slaves to plant and harvest more sugar on
them (Tomich 2004, 86–87). These developments gave rise to a debate on

the degree to which a slave-based economy could introduce technology—capital intensive and labor saving—in the production process without undermining the basis of that system. My objective is not to engage in an extensive examination of that debate but to summarize its key points.

Manuel Moreno Fraginals offered what I consider to be the strongest argument on the limits slavery imposed on the introduction of machinery and labor-saving technology in the production process. For him, no matter how important the new technologies adopted in Cuba were, they could never lead to a revolutionizing of the means of production without making the transition to wage-labor (Moreno Fraginals 1976, 40). This is because Cuba was "dealing with a quantitative change in an agricultural industry, where the relatively large labor force revolutionizes the objective conditions of the work process, although the system as such does not change. Its form is that of a production mechanism whose parts are human beings. The operation retains its manual character, depending on the strength, skill, speed, and assurance of the individual worker in handling his implement" (Moreno Fraginals 1976, 18).

Tomich took that argument to mean that although Moreno recognized that capitalism, slavery, and wage-labor coexisted in the world market and imposed its laws on slavery, the latter retained its "essential" characteristics: "Quantitative expansion is counterposed to qualitative transformation. Change within the Cuban slave economy is marked by the impossibility of revolutionizing the means of production" (Tomich 2004, 89).

Contrary to Tomich, I agree with Moreno. For him, the Cuban "sugarocracy" were slavers because "only slavery could make the initial sugar expansion possible. In Cuba, as in all colonies, there was a passionate desire for cheap and submissive labor, of a type to which our nascent capitalists could dictate conditions rather than have to submit to those labor imposed" when, for example, foreign workers arriving in Cuba either became farmers or artisans, and/or demanded higher wages than the cost of slave labor (Moreno Fraginals 1976, 131). He also compared what he called the "barbarism" of the slave system in the colonies to that of the "white slaves" in England where the "same lust for wealth gripped men of both worlds as they sought to extract the last ounce of labor" (Moreno Fraginals 1976, 132). But whereas machinery could displace workers in England, it could not do so in Cuba, especially in the cane fields.

However, after the mechanization of the mills and the transportation system, the slave system underwent a diversification in terms of the categories of unfree labor employed on the plantations. The meaning of slave labor changed to include the "pure" slave who was physically forced to work on the sugar plantations; the "hired" slave who received part of the money paid to his owner; the semi-freed slave who hired him-/herself out to his/her nominal owner and had the right to sell his/her services freely; and the salaried slave whose wages were between 50 and 70 percent of those paid to free wage-laborers. In addition to these variations, Cuba also imported labor from abroad, including from Spain, and contract labor from China to work on the large mechanized mills (Moreno Fraginals 1976, 112–13; 1985, 18–19). In other words, wage-labor relations were being mixed with those of slave labor.

The key issue for Moreno, however, was not the fact that slavery was a "typically capitalist" phenomenon whose "function was almost exclusively to produce merchandise for the world market" (Moreno Fraginals 1976, 131). It was, rather, that the changes brought to Cuba in the second half of the nineteenth century were "more economic and social than technical" despite the "significant improvements in equipment and process. But the complete renovation of the process of production was not a mere question of installing modern industrial equipment; it also implied a renovation on the social, institutional level that could not be carried out by slaveowners" (Moreno Fraginals 1985, 19).

In her response to Moreno's argument about the limits slavery imposed on revolutionizing the means of production in Cuba, Rebecca Scott, like Tomich, argues that despite the recruitment of a diversified labor force that included rented slaves, indentured Asians (mainly Chinese), and black, white, and mulatto wage workers, plantation slavery survived and production increased as "planters with capital bought vacuum pans and other modern processing apparatus, increasing the output of sugar per unit of land planted" (Scott 1985, 30–31). Some planters also resorted to renting slaves to "mitigate the problem of fixed labor costs within the system of slavery. Rental permitted the shifting of existing slave labor supply to areas of greater profitability; it did not necessarily weaken slavery as an institution" (Scott 1985, 36). Therefore, in consideration of the fact that the indentured or contract Chinese laborers were not free wage-laborers even though they were mostly concentrated in the processing sectors of the mechanized mills, she, as Tomich, concluded that this represented a challenge to the argument that "unfree labor" was incompatible with technological advancement (Scott 1985, 36).

Scott's and Tomich's point that the introduction of machinery in sugar production is not incompatible with slavery is valid, but only so long as it is understood that this technological transformation was not applied to *all* aspects of the production process but limited primarily to the transportation and milling processes where wage-laborers or contracted/indentured/rented slaves were used. Scott herself seemed to have come to the same conclusion when she admitted that the argument of an internal contradiction between slavery and revolutionizing all aspects of the production process "does contain a key insight concerning the difficulty of achieving capital-intensive development with forced labor, the maintenance expense of which must be borne year-round" (Scott 1985, 45). With that she conceded Moreno Fraginals's argument.

My main point here, then, is this. The demand for more slaves in Cuba while parts of the production process were being mechanized would seem paradoxical were it not for the fact that we are dealing with a capitalist economy based on slave labor. This is because the new technologies, while they made the transport and refining of sugar more capital intensive and profitable and increased its production, they did not alter the capital-labor relations in the cane fields that remained labor intensive. A change in the latter would have required the replacement of slave labor with wage-labor, or as happened in Cuba, a combination of slave, semi-free, and free labor with the flexibility to hire the latter on a seasonal basis.

This alternative use of labor occurred not only while slavery still existed in the region, but after its complete abolition at the end of the nineteenth century. As was the case in Cuba and in other countries like the Dominican Republic, plantation owners turned to recruiting migrant workers from other Caribbean countries like Haiti, Jamaica, and the Lesser Antilles. As Samuel Martinez pointed out, the modern sugar mills operated on a larger scale than their precursors in the slave era, but "despite improvements in milling and refining technology, the work of cutting cane remained virtually the same as it had been for centuries. As a result, the new mills demanded much greater numbers of cane cutters than had the old" (Martinez 1995, 35). But because the owners of the mills were relying on paid rather than slave labor, it was more profitable for them to recruit such workers seasonally when the sucrose content of the canes was at its highest (Martinez 1995, 35). The problem of hiring seasonal workers for the four months of the harvesting season, however, was that, as Moreno Fraginals pointed out, they would be unemployed for the other eight months. Thus, as he put it, "the modern plantation required, for its optimal running, the existence of an army of unemployed workers, ideally located off *ingenio* (estate) grounds but subjected to economic pressure that forced them to sell their services cheaply and with a minimum of social benefits, as cane cutters" (Moreno Fraginals 1976, 6; also cited in Martinez 1995, 35).

The problem for the new mill owners in the Dominican Republic and elsewhere, then, "was less one of *holding* labor on the estates than of *recapturing* it every year, after it had been released from employment during the preceding 'dead season.' . . . Only where economic need drove workers back to the sugar estates each harvest season could an adequate supply of field labor be obtained, at sufficient low cost, to feed the new mills with sugarcane" (Martinez 1995, 35, emphasis in original). Thus, just as with the unpaid labor under slavery, the use of intermediate forms of semi-free wage-labor and free wage-labor to continue to supply this new source of low-paid and seasonal labor meant that the employers could delay investing in the mechanization of the harvesting and loading processes.

As G. B. Hagelberg points out, that began to change after Puerto Rico introduced mechanical harvesters to load hand-cut canes in the 1950s, followed by the use of mechanical cane cutters in the 1960s, both of which led to a "revolution of the *entire* production process" (emphasis added). These technological innovations required changes in the layout of the fields and leveled land; changes in the drainage and irrigation systems; different planting practices such as spacing between rows; and changes in the transportation system and end-point facilities. Those operating the new machines also had to be trained and services to support and maintain those sophisticated machines had to be provided: "most importantly, cost-effective utilization of expensive mechanical equipment presupposed very different management attitudes and skills from those that had been developed to supervise large numbers of manual field workers" (Hagelberg 1985, 89). For the reasons I have outlined above, this *thorough* revolutionizing of the production process—from the planting, cutting, harvesting, transporting, and refining of sugar—could never have happened under a slave regime.

CONCLUSION

Based on the argument I have developed in this chapter, I offer the following conclusions about the relationship between capitalism and slavery. First, there is no doubt that slavery can be an integral part of the social relations of production of a global system of capitalist production of commodities for sale in a market for profit and the accumulation of capital. And second, a slave-based system of production, while highly profitable, imposes severe limits on the extent to which machinery can be substituted for workers to make the transition from absolute to relative surplus-value production in *all* aspects of the production process, as I have shown above in the case of Cuba and Puerto Rico. That is because, unlike the wage-laborer, the slave is bought and paid for by the slave master/capitalist *before* he/she engages in the production process. To displace him/her with machinery, then, would render that slave idle and hence represent a net loss in the capital invested in the original purchase since the master/capitalist must still provide for the slave's existence without getting anything in return in the form of commodities that can be sold for profit.

This is not the case with the wage-laborer. The latter is not bought whole by the employer; only his/her labor-power is, in return for a wage paid *after* he/she engages in the production process and yields commodities that are appropriated by the capitalist and sold in a market to realize the surplus value (or profit) embodied in them. Moreover, and unlike the slave, when the hired worker is not employed, the capitalist is not responsible for what happens to that worker who is left to his/her own device to provide for his/her needs. The case of the seasonal, migrant, mostly Haitian workers used in the production of sugar in the Dominican Republic illustrates that point well. In that case, the capitalists can delay investing in labor-saving technologies in certain aspects of the production process, such as in planting, cutting, and harvesting the sugarcane, as long as the supply of such seasonal labor is plentiful. That is what the uneven development of capitalist production within and between countries does: the creation of what Marx called "supernumeraries," that is, a surplus labor population or reserve army of labor "whose misery is in inverse ratio to the amount of torture it has to undergo in the form of labour" (Marx 1976, 798).

NOTES

1. Eric Williams was a prime minister of Trinidad and Tobago from 1962 to 1981. He was not a Marxist, but his book, first published in 1944, along with his *From Columbus to Castro: The History of the Caribbean 1492–1969* (1970), had a profound impact on the scholarship of the region from Marxist and other perspectives, my own included.

2. My own earlier view was similar to Pierre-Charles's. Like him, I argued then that slave relations were not capitalist because "the relationship of the direct producers to the means of

production, and the forms of surplus appropriation are different. . . . In contrast to capitalism, the slaves are neither 'separated' from the means of production, nor receive a wage in return for their labor. Slaves, as the property of their master, are objectively bound to the means of production, and they do not enter into any contractual relationship with their owner" (Dupuy 1981, 7).

3. By "extra-economic" compulsion Marx and Marxists generally mean the appropriation of surplus from the direct producers by "noneconomic" means, such as in the case of serfdom, slavery, coerced cash-crop labor where the laborers are compelled (by force or obligation) to work for their lord or master.

4. As I will explain below, the hyphen in *world-system* or *world-economy* is because Wallerstein takes it as the unit of analysis, and not the nation-states, that goes through different "stages" of historical development, as he argues Marx and Marxist theorists do.

5. Wallerstein's argument here is in reference to those Marxist theorists/historians, Robert Brenner among them, who were engaged in the debate on the "transition" from feudalism to capitalism in western Europe initiated by Maurice Dobb and Paul Sweezy in the late 1940s to early 1950s and continued in the 1970s. Essentially that debate focused on the factors that played the most "revolutionary role" in in the dissolution of the old feudal property relations and the creation of capitalist property relations of production, principally a proletariat or wage-labor force considered to be the *sine qua non* for the development of capitalism. Whereas Dobb (1978a, 1978b, 1978c) focused on the dynamics within western Europe, England in particular, that led to the transformation of the feudal relations, Sweezy (1978a, 1978b) emphasized the role of long-distance trade associated with European colonialism in engendering a system of commodity production for the market in western Europe that ultimately led to the demise of the feudal system and the development of capitalism. Those interested in that debate see *The Transition from Feudalism to Capitalism* (Hilton 1978).

6. For an alternative, and more compelling, analysis of the differences between Venetian, Dutch, and English capitalism/imperialism in the early modern era, see Giovanni Arrighi (2001).

7. The argument that ideologies of racial or cultural inferiority are "noncommercial" and "extra-economic" does not hold. Ideologies of racial inferiority, and the rankings assigned to different groups largely based on differences in skin color, with whites at the top, blacks at the bottom, and other categories in between, did not exist before the sixteenth century. They were developed subsequent to the colonization of the New World and the enslavement of both its indigenous populations and of Africans brought there simultaneously with the rise of the capitalist world economy in the sixteenth century. See my discussion of these ideological deployments/formulations in ch. 1 of *Haiti: From Revolutionary Slaves to Powerless Citizens* (Dupuy 2014).

8. Wood could have been more convincing here had she argued that while New World slavery was a product of and thus a relation of the capitalist world economy, it nonetheless conflicted with its ideological claim of being the purveyor of liberty and equality for all. This claim may be veiled with regard to wage-labor because, as Marx pointed out, though nominally free, the wage-laborer, having been expropriated from having independent access to his/her means of production and reproduction, is in fact compelled to sell his/her labor-power to a capitalist in return for a wage in order to survive. Despite this unfreedom and the unequal relation between the wage-laborer and the capitalist, workers have the ability—and at least in those societies with democratic structures, the right—to organize and to struggle for their interests against those of the capitalist. And though the playing field is uneven, stacked against them, and never fully guaranteed, workers sometimes succeed in doing so without having to resort to a full-scale revolution. In the New World slave societies, however, such claims and

possibilities were a non sequitur. The slave was property and had no rights. By contrast those who were freed (e.g., the free blacks and people of color or mulattoes) such as in Saint-Domingue and the other French colonies in the Caribbean, could and did struggle to gain rights vis-à-vis whites—including the right to own slaves. No such alternative existed for the slaves, leaving revolution as their only option—or fleeing into *marronage*—if they were not to wait for their masters or their governments to grant it to them on their own time. Even though slaves rebelled in most of the colonies of the Americas (e.g., Hispaniola, Jamaica, Dutch Guiana, Martinique, Mexico, Colombia, Venezuela, Brazil, and the United States; see Genovese 1979), only in Saint-Domingue were they successful in bringing down the slave system and winning their freedom outright. In the United States, it took a civil war to win the slaves their freedom, but it was a war initiated from above by competing factions of the US ruling class over the issue of slavery rather than from below by the slaves themselves as happened in Saint-Domingue.

9. For Marx, surplus value is created when, in a working day of a specified length of time, the worker works beyond the *necessary labor time* to produce commodities that are equal to the wages paid to the worker by the capitalist, and during which he/she produces more commodities of equal value but for which he/she is not paid. That second part of the working day constitutes the *surplus labor time* and yields the *surplus value* appropriated by the capitalist. Marx then explained the concepts of *absolute* and *relative* surplus value thusly: the former is the name given to the "value produced by lengthening the working day," whereas the latter refers to the shortening of the "necessary labor-time, and from the curtailment of the necessary labor-time, and from the corresponding alteration in the respective lengths of the two components of the working day." The production of relative surplus value, then, implies an increase in the productivity of the worker and a corresponding fall in the relative value of the laborer (Marx 1976, 432). Put differently, relative surplus value consists of an increase in the exploitation of the laborer whereby the necessary labor time is shortened and the surplus labor time increases while the length of the working day remains constant.

10. This section is taken in part from Dupuy (1989, esp. ch. 1).

11. For a more detailed analysis of the Spanish conquest of Haiti, see Dupuy (1976).

12. The term *Creole* refers to those born in the colony and included white men, "free people of color," generically referred to as mulattoes, but also blacks and their descendants.

13. It may be true, as I also wrote, that slavery *sensu stricto* is not capitalist (Dupuy 1989, 22) because it can and has existed independently of that system. But that clearly is not the case when it is an integral part of the capitalist system in which the slave relations were embedded in the New World since the sixteenth century.

14. As Hall also points out, however, when the African slave trade could no longer be relied upon to replenish the slave population, slave-breeding was encouraged if not actually forced in the United States especially, where the "slave system enjoyed very favorable conditions for the procreation of an American-born slave population during the nineteenth century" (Hall 1971, 153).

Chapter Two

Masters, Slaves, and Revolution in Saint-Domingue

A Critique of the Hegelian Interpretation

Georg Wilhelm Friedrich Hegel's iconic master-slave "life-and-death struggle" dialectic developed in *The Phenomenology of Mind (1807)* (1967) made its way into analyses of the singular and Atlantic world-shaking slave revolution of Saint-Domingue of 1791–1804. Many writers have made references to Hegel's argument in discussing African slavery in Africa and the New World in general.[1] But the authors I will consider here, Pierre-Franklin Tavares (1992) and Susan Buck-Morss (2009), attempted to show that Hegel derived his hypothesis specifically from the slave uprising in Saint-Domingue, whereas for Nick Nesbitt (2004) it was Hegel's argument on "Absolute Freedom and Terror," also in the *Phenomenology*, that was inspired by that singular revolution. This was the case even if all three authors admit that Hegel himself never referred to that revolution specifically in his texts.

Hegel knew and wrote about the French Revolution of 1789, with which the Saint-Domingue Revolution was directly related. But he never mentioned that connection and also remained silent on the fact that the slaves of Saint-Domingue defeated the expeditionary army that his hero, Napoleon Bonaparte, sent there in 1802 to crush the uprising, an omission that Tavares commented on as well (Tavares 1992, 115). Bonaparte's brother-in-law, General Victoire Emmanuel Leclerc, led that expedition and succeeded in arresting and deporting Toussaint Louverture to France. Leclerc, whose objective was to exterminate all the blacks and start over in Saint-Domingue by importing new slaves from Africa who had never known slavery or revolted against it in the New World, succumbed to yellow fever in 1802. He was succeeded by General Donatien Rochambeau, but he fared no better than his predecessor in defeating the revolutionary forces despite his penchant for cruelty. In fact, his brutality had the opposite effect. It led the mulatto forces under the leadership of Alexandre Pétion to realize that their own freedom and survival depended on uniting with the black forces under the leadership of Jean-Jacques Dessalines rather than fighting against them as they did when, led by André Rigaud, they launched an unsuccessful civil war against Louverture in 1799 (Dubois 2004, 290–96; Fick 1990, 220–36). The united forces went on to defeat the French, declared the colony's independence on January 1, 1804, and renamed it Haiti, which was its original precolonial Arawakan name of Ayiti. Hegel's silences notwithstanding, Tavares, Buck-Morss, and Nesbitt insist that his concept of the master-slave life-and-death struggle *had to be* derived from the Saint-Domingue Revolution.

But if Hegel never talked about Saint-Domingue, he did mention Haiti once. Tavares and Buck-Morss cite Hegel's passage in the 1827–1828 *Philosophy of Subjective Spirit, Volume 2: Anthropology* (Hegel 1978) where, in talking about the lack of interest and the "state of undisturbed naivety" among "Negroes," he noted that they nonetheless "cannot be said to be ineducable, for not only have they occasionally received Christianity with the greatest thankfulness and spoken movingly of the freedom they have gained from it after prolonged spiritual servitude, but in Haiti they have even formed a state on Christian principle" (Hegel 1978, 54–55; Buck-Morss 2009, 62n119; Tavares 1992, 113). Hegel, however, immediately qualified that statement in the sentence that followed: "They show no inner tendency to culture, however. In their homeland the most shocking despotism prevails; there, they have no feeling for the personality of man, their spirit is quite dormant, remains sunk within itself, makes no progress, and so corresponds to the compact and *undifferentiated* mass of the African terrain" (Hegel 1978, 54–55. emphasis in original). Neither Tavares nor Buck-Morss referred to or commented on that passage.

Contrary to these three authors, I will argue that Hegel could not possibly have derived his theory of the master-slave dialectic from the Saint-Domingue Revolution, for two main reasons. The first, as the sentences quoted from him above suggest, has to do with his racism. To be sure, Tavares, Buck-Morss, and Nesbitt acknowledge Hegel's racism, but they see it as incidental and not fundamental to his argument about the master-slave relation. I do, because Hegel himself made it fundamental to his views on history and human, social, and political development. As one among many other European Enlightenment thinkers, such as François Marie Arouet Voltaire, Charles Louis de Secondat Baron de Montesquieu, David Hume, Immanuel Kant, Thomas Jefferson in the United States, and Moreau de Saint-Méry in Saint-Domingue, Hegel believed that Africans were savages and inherently inferior to white Europeans. Consequently, I will show, even though he considered slavery in general to be unjust, he justified the enslavement of Africans by Europeans in the New World colonies of the Americas as a means of raising them above their savagery.

By contrast, the master and slave depicted in the *Phenomenology of Mind (1807)* (Hegel 1967), and before that in the *System of Ethical Life (1802/3) and First Philosophy of Spirit (Part III of the System of Speculative Philosophy 1803/4)* (Hegel 1979), are both individuals coming out of the state of nature seeking mutual recognition from one another, and who, as Alex Honneth suggested, already had "accepted the other in advance as a partner to interaction upon whom they are willing to allow their own activity to be dependent" (Honneth 1995, 45). They engage in a life-and-death struggle, but realizing that they cannot annihilate one another, they "sublate" their extreme terms in such a way that the one who was willing to risk his life became master, and the other, fearing death, submitted to the stronger combatant and became the bondsman or slave. Even though this relationship is one of inequality and domination, the slave understood that he/she needed to be free and recognized as an equal and does so through his/her labor. For Hegel, however, since the black African is a savage who never emerged from the state of nature, is immature, has no concept of freedom, and deserved to be enslaved, it follows logically that he/she would be ipso facto excluded as a candidate for the struggle for mutual recognition.

The second and related reason is that, contrary to Hegel's allegory about the struggle for mutual recognition between the master and the slave, the real master-slave relation in Saint-Domingue had nothing to do with recognition, either on the part of the master vis-à-vis the slave, or on the part of the slave vis-à-vis the master through his/her labor. Rather, that relationship had to do with the brutal exploitation of the slave by the master to extract the maximum surplus value (profit) from him/her in the shortest time possible, and to replace him/her with a new slave when he/she died, a fact that compelled plantation owners in Saint-Domingue to renew their slave population every ten years on average (see ch. 1). For his/her part, the slave was not interested in recognizing the master, or in being recognized by him, but rather wanted to liberate him-/herself from the latter by any means possible. In Saint-Domingue, the slaves did exactly that in their revolution.

Thus, while Hegel may have been silent on Saint-Domingue in particular, he was quite vocal on slavery in Africa and the New World colonies in general. Tavares, Buck-Morss, and Nesbitt did not consider that Hegel's racism had anything to do with his depiction of *who* qualified to participate in his life-and-death struggle allegory, but, believing that such a struggle *had* to have real-life candidates, they went searching for their hero in the Saint-Domingue Revolution. Hegel did not make that easy for them, however, so they had to settle for allusions, as Sibylle Fisher pointed out (2004, 27). For Tavares, Hegel's silences meant that one is led to conclude that either Hegel was really ignorant of events in Saint-Domingue and Haiti, in which case he would have developed his argument on self-consciousness and the life-and-death struggle between master and slave fictively, or he knew and hence grounded his analysis historically (Tavares 1992, 118). For her part, Buck-Morss is adamant that "we cannot think Hegel *without* Haiti" (Buck-Morss 2009, 16; emphasis in original). But then she, too, hesitated: "If it is indisputable that Hegel knew about Haiti, as did indeed the entire European reading public, why is there not more explicit discussion in his texts?" (Buck-Morss 2009, 17). She answered, by way of Tavares, who had drawn on the work of Jacques d'Hondt—who did not refer to Saint-Domingue either—to argue that Hegel's silences were due to his affiliations with Freemasonry and their tendency to guard their sources of documentation closely and not reveal them. As she put it, "one cannot help but be struck by the affinities between the politics of Hegel's early philosophy of spirit, and his reading of the journal *Minerva* with its Mason-spirited endorsement of Girondin cosmopolitanism committed to the international spread of revolutionary ideals, explicitly including Toussaint L'Ouverture's republic, yet critical of what Hegel in the *Phenomenology* called the 'abstract negation' of revolutionary terror" (Buck-Morss 2009, 18). She also noted that Hegel was completing *The Phenomenology of Mind* at the same time that Napoleon Bonaparte's army invaded Germany, shelled and occupied the city of Jena, ransacked Hegel's house, and messed up his papers. This was reason enough, Buck-Morss contended, for Hegel not to mention the slave rebellion in Saint-Domingue directly in the manuscript to avoid political persecution (2009, 20). Further, in discussing Hegel's rush and risk of moving to Bamberg in March 1807 to take a job with the *Bamberger Zeitung* newspaper, which was very sympathetic to Napoleon, Buck-Morss wondered about sections that were missing from Hegel's 1803 manuscript *System of Ethical Life (1802/3) and First Philosophy of Spirit* and the motives of Hegel's posthumous editors in deciding which materials to include in his work (Buck-Morss 2009, 20).

It is worth noting, however, that in a letter he wrote to his friend Friedrich Niethammer, Hegel said that he had completed the *Phenomenology of Spirit* (or of *Mind*) the night before the Battle of Jena and that he had sent the last remaining pages of the book by special courier to his publisher, and personally took the remaining pages of the book with him so they would not get lost (Pinkard 2000, 229–30; Butler and Seiler 1984, 113). Moreover, according to Terry Pinkard, Hegel's biographer, when Hegel assumed the editorship of the *Bamberger Zeitung*, he was expected not to express his own political views, but his admiration for Napoleon and what he believed the French were doing in Germany made it impossible for him not to do so. He went as far as denouncing what he thought were the lies of the official Prussian accounts of Napoleon's maneuvers and juxtaposing them with accounts from other newspapers he considered more flattering or accurate. As Pinkard noted, it was "abundantly clear" that the newspaper's pro-Napoleon slant "was fully in line with Hegel's own opinion; he was in no way catering to the reigning authorities and censors of Bavaria against his own wishes or his own ideas" (Pinkard 2000, 247). It seems, then, that if, as Buck-Morss suggested, Hegel had lost his courage when Napoleon's army marched into Jena in October 1806, he had regained it several months later in 1807 when he defied the Prussian authorities.

Be that as it may, Buck-Morss, in a similar vein to Tavares, insisted that Hegel derived his master-slave dialectic from his knowledge of the Saint-Domingue revolution: "Either Hegel was the blindest of all blind philosophers of freedom in Enlightenment Europe, surpassing Locke and Rousseau by far in his ability to block out reality right in front of his nose or Hegel knew—knew about real slaves revolting successfully against real masters, and he elaborated his dialectic of lordship and bondage deliberately within this contemporary context" (Buck-Morss 2009, 50). As I mentioned above, Sibylle Fisher justifiably questioned Buck-Morss's certainty when she wrote that she (Buck-Morss) was "inviting us as readers of the *Phenomenology* to supply the historical references we routinely supply when Hegel appears to be alluding to the French Revolution or Napoleon." It also could well be, Fisher added, that it is we who might be reluctant or refuse to "consider the possibility of [Hegel's] allusion to Haiti," but "we may wonder whether

[Buck-Morss] is not asking us to do more than just acknowledge an allusion" (Fisher 2004, 27).

For his part, Nick Nesbitt admitted that Hegel never actually referred to Haiti. But he argues nonetheless that contrary to those who have interpreted Hegel's chapter "Absolute Freedom and Terror" in the *Phenomenology* as a critique of the period between 1792 and 1794 in France under the Jacobin dictatorship and the Terror, it was in fact referring to the Saint-Domingue revolution, where "its violence reached unimagined heights of brutality on both sides, that an entire society was literally reduced to ashes in the name of a single imperative: universal emancipation" (Nesbitt 2004, 18, 23). He went on to interpret Hegel's discussion of the "*actualization* of human freedom as a universal emancipation from servitude" in the *Philosophy of Right* as being derived from the experience of the Saint-Domingue Revolution. But he did not offer a shred of evidence from either of those two works to support his claims (Nesbitt 2004, 26–27).

Nesbitt, even more than Buck-Morss and Tavares, is grasping at straws here. Contrary to his silences on the Saint-Domingue Revolution, Hegel was quite vocal and very clear on his views of the French Revolution and its Terror. As J. B. Baillie (translator of the *Phenomenology*) noted, Hegel was referring "to the *régime* under the French revolutionaries" (Baillie, in Hegel 1967, 599n1). Pinkard also pointed out that Hegel considered the French Revolution to be the "decisive modern event" that put forth the concept of "absolute freedom" as its ultimate objective (Pinkard 2000, 213). According to Hegel, this "undivided substance of absolute freedom puts itself on the throne of the world, without any power being able to offer effectual resistance." By this he meant that all the social distinctions and "division [of society] into separate social spheres collapsed into a single whole," and, as a result, that "all social ranks or classes, which are the component spiritual factors into which the whole is differentiated, are effaced and annulled" (Hegel 1967, 601).

Given that to be the case, there were no longer any institutions to "mediate the claim to 'absolute freedom' embodied in the revolutionary upheaval . . . no group in the Revolution could establish itself as anything other than just another particular point of view, just another 'faction.'" At this point the "Revolution became the Terror, with the sanitized execution of the guillotine serving to protect the 'whole' from those who supposedly threatened it" (cited in Pinkard 2000, 213). When that happened, universal freedom could only give rise to "the rage and fury of destruction," and therefore becomes "*death*—a death that achieves nothing with no more significance than cleaving a head of cabbage or swallowing a draught of water" (Hegel 1967, 604–5).

For Pinkard, Hegel's stance on the violence of the French Revolution showed his Girondist sympathies when he wrote to Schelling that the execution of Carrier[2] by the revolutionary government "revealed the complete ignominy of Robespierre's party" (Pinkard 2000, 54; see also Butler and Seiler 1984, 29; D'Hondt 1989, 129). As Rebecca Comay pointed out, for Hegel the French Revolution represented a turning point for modernity, which "takes ruination as its foundation" (Comay 2010, 59). Thus, Hegel saw the Terror as "the return of a repressed fanaticism. Terror marks the modern crisis of secularization: it expresses the vicissitudes of a superstition that had been insulted, assaulted, and persecuted and thereby prolonged, exaggerated, and perverted by a rationality blind to its own reasons and above all to its fascinated complicity with its victims" (Comay 2010, 60).

Jürgen Habermas offered one of the most poignant critiques of Hegel's treatment of the French Revolution. Hegel, he argues, "celebrates the revolution because he fears it; Hegel elevates the revolution to the primary principle of philosophy for the sake of a philosophy which is to overcome the revolution" (Habermas 1973, 121). The gist of his argument focused on the distinction between the concept of abstract right, which Hegel legitimized in terms of world history, from the actual rights produced by the revolution, or, put differently, "he separates the abstract freedom which has gained positive assertion in bourgeois society (Code Napoléon) from that abstract freedom which wishes to actualize itself (Robespierre)" (Habermas 1973, 121). Looked at yet another way, when actual rights become entangled with the subjective concept or consciousness of absolute freedom, they confront their weakness. Thus, Hegel understands the Terror from the "negation of absolute freedom exaggerated to the point of absolute freedom. It is toward this that the critique of the French Revolution is directed" (Habermas 1973, 123).

This revulsion to the actual realization of abstract freedom by the revolution explains why Hegel welcomed the rise of Napoleon Bonaparte to power after he defeated Robespierre and ushered in the new bourgeois order embodied in the Code Napoleon (Habermas 1973, 123). Pinkard made the same point: Hegel welcomed Bonaparte's rise to power after the fall of Robespierre because he saw him as the person who would "finish the 'novel' of the French Revolution" and put the "abstract ideals of modern freedom in practice" (Pinkard 2000, 213). Similarly, Jacques D'Hondt concluded that for

Hegel the revolution was finished, as was history, because after it all other religions would converge toward Christianity as the fundamental religion. Economic liberalism would also "function quietly . . . [and] the bourgeois republic or constitutional monarchy," which is not "a stage, after others, but mankind's political culmination," would lead it to "imagine that nothing else is possible" (D'Hondt 1989, 130).

But it was not only in France that Hegel saw Napoleon as the embodiment of modernity and enlightenment. Admiring him as "this world-soul—riding astride a horse reaches out across the world and conquers it" (Butler and Seiler 1984, 114), Hegel also welcomed his invasion of Germany because he believed that he would introduce the necessary reforms to bring Germany into the modern world. As he wrote in a letter to Niethammer on August 29, 1807, "Everyone here awaits the reorganization [of Germany] to break upon us. There is, moreover, talk of a great assembly of the princes and magistrates of the Empire. The crucial decision will surely come from Paris" (Butler and Seiler 1984, 140). As Pinkard pointed out, all the debates taking place in Germany about "which states were sovereign and which old rights remained in force, and about whether the Confederation of the Rhine was the successor of the Holy Roman Empire were all, to Hegel, simply absurd and beside the point" (Pinkard 2000, 254). In that same letter, Hegel went on to say, "The German professors of constitutional law have not stopped spewing forth masses of writings on the concept of sovereignty and the meaning of the Acts of Confederation. The great professor of constitutional law sits in Paris. The German princes have neither grasped the concept of a free monarchy yet nor sought to make it real. Napoleon will have to sort all this" (Butler and Seiler 1984, 141; Pinkard 2000, 254). To Hegel, Pinkard pointed out, all that "was really efficacious in the modern world, what ultimately had a purchase on people's minds and hearts was the emerging inevitable structure of modern life itself" (Pinkard 2000, 254).

The defeat of Napoleon by the British in 1814, his return to France after escaping from Elba in 1815, and his ultimate defeat and surrender at Waterloo in June 1815 were undoubtedly unwelcome and disturbing news to Hegel. He hoped nonetheless that the modernizing reforms Napoleon brought to Germany would not be reversed (Pinkard 2000, 285–87, 307–11; Butler and Seiler 1984, 365, 602). In a letter he had written to Niethammer on April 29, 1814, Hegel said that there was "nothing more *tragic* [than] to see a great genius destroy himself." Nonetheless, Hegel interpreted Napoleon's defeat as being in keeping with his character, which had also led to his successes. And, referring to the section on "Absolute Freedom and Terror" in the *Phenomenology of Mind*, he said he had predicted "Napoleon's downfall because of his belief (which he still held) that the 'novel of the revolution' would not be finished in France but in Germany" (Pinkard 2000, 311; Butler and Seiler 1984, 306–8).

AN ALTERNATIVE INTERPRETATION

In my view, then, Hegel's focus in his texts (and letters, where he often explained what he meant) was in interpreting the transformations taking place in Europe, France and Germany in particular, and in engaging with the major philosophical figures and debates of his time. Thus, the fact that he remained silent on the Saint-Domingue Revolution should not be surprising since it played no role in the formulation or development of his ideas, notwithstanding his one and only superficial and racist claim that the "Negroes" of Haiti could perhaps come out of their cultural darkness by embracing Christianity.

It is true, as Tavares noted, that Saint-Domingue was still a French colony and not yet an independent state when Hegel remarked that "in Haiti they have even formed a state on Christian principle." Toussaint Louverture did indeed create the 1801 constitution that proclaimed Roman Catholicism as the only religion to be observed in the colony.[3] As Beaubrun Ardouin noted, however, that constitution was virtually taken from the one proclaimed by the colonial assembly of Saint-Marc in May 1790, which, in turn, had been adapted from the colonial doctrine issued by the colonialists in the North, both of which aimed at self-government for the colony (Ardouin 1958, 4:76). But insofar as Hegel relied strictly on that official pronouncement, his statement was not prima facie wrong even if he confused the colony under Toussaint's rule with the actual State of Haiti. As always, facts on the ground and the divisions and conflicts that characterized the colony, or what Marx called the many determinations that express concrete reality, tell a different story.

Toussaint's constitution established a de facto state by declaring, among other clauses, that while it remained a French colony, slavery was forever abolished and that all individuals born in the colony were free and French; that discrimination on the basis of color in employment was prohibited; that Roman Catholicism was the only religion to be observed; that religious and civil marriage were protected and divorce was not recognized; and that the colony was to be governed by the laws proposed by the governor and ratified by a central assembly (Ardouin 1958, 4:76–77; Janvier 1886, 8–10). Such an act, combined with the letter Toussaint wrote to Bonaparte in February 1801 to let him know who was now in charge of the colony, amounted to nothing less than a declaration of war against the latter. As I noted in the previous chapter, though he would later regret that decision, Bonaparte responded to Louverture in short order by sending a massive military expedition comprising some 408 warships and 80,000 troops to crush him and the revolution (Dupuy 1989, 53, 67).

It is worth noting that this decision came as the French forces were facing defeat by the British in Egypt and they were forced to leave that same year. Bonaparte had seen the conquest of Egypt (in 1798) as necessary to establish a French colony on the Nile that would "prosper without slaves" (Bonaparte 1946, 350), and

> would afford such a market for our manufactures as would produce a great benefit in every branch of our industry; and we should soon be called upon to supply all the wants of the inhabitants of the desert of Africa, Abyssinia, Arabia, and a great part of Syria. These people are destitute of everything; and what are Saint-Domingo and all our colonies compared to such a vast region? France, in return, would obtain from Egypt wheat, rice, sugar, nitre, and all the productions of Africa and Asia. (Bonaparte 1946, 350)

Having their own imperialist objectives in mind, however, the British were determined to deprive the French of that prize and succeeded in doing so. Retaking Saint-Domingue from Louverture and reestablishing slavery there, then, became an imperative. General Leclerc, who led the French expedition to Saint-Domingue, succeeded in arresting and deporting Louverture to France, but the revolutionary forces reorganized, renewed their offensives, and defeated Napoleon's army.

If Hegel followed events in Saint-Domingue/Haiti, he had to know about that expedition and its defeat, as well as Bonaparte's defeat and retreat from Egypt. But he said nothing about either of them. For those like Tavares, Buck-Morss, and Nesbitt who are certain that Hegel derived his master-slave dialectic on the Saint-Domingue Revolution, his silence must be especially perplexing, leading Tavares to ask how can we "understand why Hegel restricted the activities of his hero solely to the European theater?" (Tavares 1992, 114–15). As I will argue below, however, given Hegel's view of Africans as savages who never emerged from the state of nature, their decisive defeat of his hero was understandably more than he could countenance.

Toussaint's embrace of Catholicism notwithstanding, Vodou, derived from the various spiritual, healing, and cultural practices the slaves brought with them from their respective African homelands (Senegambia, the Windward Coast, the Gold Coast, the Bight of Benin, the Bight of Biafra, West Central African Kongo, and Angola), was the religion of the vast majority of the slaves, intertwined as it became since the seventeenth century with elements borrowed from Catholicism (Dayan 1995; Desmangles 1992; Fick 1990; Hurbon 2009; Ramsey 2011).[4] As Jean Fouchard has shown, however, the colonial authorities forbade its practice and tried to suppress it. To that end, Catholicism, which the Code Noir (Articles 1–3) had declared the only religion to be allowed, taught to, and practiced by the slaves in the colony (Sala-Molin 1987, 85–91), became a means to "mollify the slave, to lead him to submit to his masters and to the colonial ferocity and its revolting situation" (Fouchard 1953, 44; see also Fick 1990, 65).

But forcing the practice of Vodou to go underground also offered the slaves a space in which they could contemplate and plot their various strategies of resistance (such as poisoning their masters), and form bands of maroons who could raid and set fire to the plantations, all of which foreshadowed the general uprising that would lead to independence in 1804 (Fouchard 1953, 27). In itself, Fouchard maintained, Vodou may not contain an ideology of liberation or have played a decisive role in the general uprising and the struggle for independence. But neither can it be denied that it provided a space to prepare for and contribute to the atmosphere favorable to the uprising (Fouchard 1953, 36). Vertus Saint-Louis made a similar point when he suggested that, as an element in the "daily imaginary of the slave," Vodou "must have been present throughout the course of the revolution without having been necessarily a cause" (Saint-Louis 2008, 163).

After Haiti declared its independence, the first constitution it issued in 1805 did not recognize a dominant religion but proclaimed the separation of church and state; that all cults could be observed; and that the right to divorce and civil marriage were recognized, all of which represented a clear defiance of Rome. Jean-Jacques Dessalines, who formed the first government of independent Haiti and made himself emperor, was assassinated in 1806. A civil war broke out between the forces loyal to Henri Christophe, who proclaimed himself king and created the State of Haiti in the north, and those loyal to Alexandre Pétion, who formed the Republic of Haiti in the west and south. The constitution of 1806 issued by Pétion declared Catholicism as the state religion, but also allowed for other religions to be observed as well, including

Vodou and Protestant cults. In the north, Christophe, unable to get the Vatican to send an archbishop to officiate his coronation, encouraged the spread of Anglicanism and Methodism as a way to break with French influence. Still, those faiths could not be observed publicly. After the reunification of Haiti by Jean-Pierre Boyer in 1818 in the south and west, and in the rest of the country after Christophe's death by suicide in 1820, the Vatican, insisting that Catholicism had to be the only religion observed, refused to send priests to the country, "resulting in an open schism between the Haitian state and Rome which lasted for fifty-six years" (Desmangles 1992, 42–43).

Even though the Vatican signed a concordat in 1860 with the government of Fabre-Nicholas Geffrard, it was generally the case that the divided and quarreling ruling factions who succeeded one another throughout the nineteenth century and well into the twentieth tended to embrace Catholicism. Though here and there this or that ruling faction either tolerated or was hostile to the practice of Vodou, the state in Haiti as a whole was "constantly confronted with the dominance of the beliefs and practices of Vodou in all social sectors, but more specifically among the peasantry" (Hurbon 2009, 201). Thus, while religious ideologies and observances are not class specific, it remains the case that in Haiti since independence, and before that as a French colony, religion and class tended to correlate positively. Again, as Fouchard put it, Haiti's elites, in their attachment to their Christian, European, and bourgeois values, considered Vodou repugnant and "condemn it as a gross superstition or some inherited defect that is best forgotten" (Fouchard 1953, 35). Fouchard here was referring to the foundational economic, political, and cultural contradictions that have divided Haitian society since the time of Toussaint Louverture: those between the emerging ruling class that took control of the colony with Toussaint and the state after independence— regardless of which warring faction, mulatto or black, controlled it at any one time—and the various ideologies they deployed to promote the interests of their class against those of the majority of the population.[5]

Those who claim that Hegel "knew" about the Saint-Domingue Revolution and developed his master-slave dialectic from it might not expect him to know or care much about what happened in Haiti after it became independent. But, if indeed he "knew" about Saint-Domingue, and given the central role that religion played in his oeuvre, one would have expected him to show a greater mastery of the role that it played in the conflicts that unfolded in the colony and its revolution. The brief and racist passage his advocates cited from him reveals instead that he was profoundly misinformed. Or, if he knew, then he chose to ignore those facts to make his claim that embracing Christianity—which as I have indicated, was a principal ideological arsenal in the oppression of the slaves—was the gateway to freedom and civilization for those African souls. This was a view shared by many among Haiti's ruling class, starting with Toussaint Louverture himself who, as Adeleke Adeeko remarked, tried "hard to make Haiti into a tropical France" (Adeeko 2005, 12).[6]

Buck-Morss claimed—and Nesbitt agreed—that Hegel "was perhaps always a cultural racist if not a biological one," and went on to ask whether his racist views of African culture and post-revolutionary Haiti had not led him to "reconsider Haiti's 'great experiment.' But what is clear is that in an effort to become more erudite in African studies during the 1820s, Hegel was in fact becoming dumber" (Buck-Morss 2009, 69–73; Nesbitt 2004, 31n9). Those contentions do not hold, however. Hegel did not suddenly become a racist when he supposedly "moved away from Haiti" in the 1820s. He began to formulate his views on race in his *Lectures on the History of Philosophy*, between 1816 and 1830, which were published as *The Philosophy of History* (1830–1831) (1956); in the *Lectures on the Philosophy of World History* (1822–1828 and 1830) (1975); in the *Lectures on the Philosophy of Spirit 1827–28* (2007); and in the *Philosophy of Subjective Spirit*, which Tavares and Buck-Morss used as their only "evidence" that he knew something about Saint-Domingue/Haiti, and which was based on lectures he delivered between 1820 and 1830 (1978). This was thus long after Toussaint Louverture's constitution and at the time that Buck-Morss said Hegel was becoming dumber, rather than in his earlier lectures or in the 1807 *Phenomenology*, whence he allegedly developed his master-slave dialectic but never mentioned Haiti or Saint-Domingue.

Hegel was part of a long succession of Enlightenment thinkers who, since the late seventeenth to the nineteenth centuries, sought to elaborate ideologies of racial superiority and inferiority based on physical and phenotypical characteristics (such as facial features, skull shape and size, skin color, hair texture) to rank the different groups of human beings, primarily along differences of skin color, on a hierarchical continuum with whites at the top, blacks at the bottom, and other categories in between. The development of these ideologies was intimately linked to the expansion of western Europe, the colonization of the Americas, the genocidal extermination of the indigenous populations, and the rape of Africa and enslavement of Africans.

Among them were major figures such as Voltaire, Locke, Hume, Kant, Montesquieu, and Jefferson, as mentioned previously.

A few examples will suffice. In *De l'Esprit des Lois* (1748), after arguing why the enslavement of Africans was necessary for the well-being of the colonies, Montesquieu proclaimed that the slaves "are black from head to toe; their nose is so flattened that it is almost impossible to pity them. It cannot be thought that God, who is so wise, could have put a soul, especially a good soul, in such a body so completely black. [It] is impossible to suppose that these people could be men, because if we suppose them to be men, we would start to believe that we ourselves are not Christians" (Montesquieu 1973, I:265). In his *Essai sur les mœurs et l'esprit des nations*, written between 1745 and 1778, Voltaire claimed that the "black race is a species of men different from ours, as the race of spaniels is from the greyhound. [T]he form of their eyes [and] their wooly hair in no way resembles ours, and one could say that if their intelligence is not different from ours as we understand it, it is far inferior. They are incapable of great attention. They believe they were born in Guinea to be sold to whites and to serve them" (Voltaire 1963, 2:305–6).

In "Of National Characters," Hume, after seemingly rejecting a physiological explanation for differences among human beings, nonetheless excluded Africans from that generalization: "I am apt to suspect the negroes to be naturally inferior to the whites. There scarcely ever was a civilized nation of that complexion, nor even any individual, eminent either in action or speculation. No ingenious manufactures among them, *no arts, no sciences*" (Hume 1742, note [M], 222, emphasis in original). In "Observations on the Feelings of the Beautiful and the Sublime," Kant, after comparing Arabs, Persians, Japanese, Indians, and Chinese to Europeans in terms of their moral, aesthetic, religious, and intellectual predispositions, argues that "the Negroes of Africa have by nature no feeling, which rises above the toiling. So essential is the differences between these two races of men [whites and blacks], and it appears to be equally great with regard to their mental capacities, as with regard to the color" (Kant 1799, 73), And, in "Notes on the State of Virginia," published in 1787, Thomas Jefferson wrote about the differences between whites and blacks by observing that "whether the black of the negro resides in the reticular membrane between the skin and the scarf-skin, or in the scarf-skin itself; whether it proceeds from the color of the blood, the color of the bile, or from that of some other secretion, the difference is fixed in nature, and is as real as if its seat and cause were better known to us. I advance it therefore that the blacks, whether originally a distinct race, or made different by time and circumstances, are inferior to the whites in the endowments of both body and mind" (Jefferson 1984, 264, 267, 270).

There is no such thing as a "cultural" racist who is not also a "biological" racist, even if the latter was not codified until the nineteenth century under the cloak of "science" to do what ideological (cultural, religious) formulations had already done: whites were the superior "race" and black Africans were at the bottom of the heap with other categories in between (Malik 1996, 84–100). As Mbembe noted, Hegel represented the "culmination of the gregarious moment of Western thinking," which "propelled by imperialist impulse represented the Black Man as the prototype of a prehuman figure incapable of emancipating itself from bestiality, of reproducing itself, or of raising itself up to the level of its god. Locked within sensation, the Black Man struggled to break the chains of biological necessity and for that reason was unable to take a truly human form and shape his own world" (Mbembe 2017, 17).

In discussing the continental divisions of the world in his *Lectures on the Philosophy of Spirit 1827–28* (2007), Hegel opined that the terrestrial differences among them were "connected with the different natural determinations of humans." He then claimed that there were four races: the American, which though containing different varieties of people, contrasted with that of the Old World, wherein the African character was very different, as was the Asiatic from the European. He divided the African continent between North Africa, which had more of a European character similar to the Near East, and sub-Saharan Africa (Hegel 2007, 88). He then went on to put forth a physiological and climatic theory of race that was also being espoused by some of his contemporaries such as Barthold Niebuhr, for example. "As we know," Hegel argues, "the effects and influence of climate are extremely variable. The differences of races are therefore in part merely physiological; here belong differences of color" (Hegel 2007, 88). It followed for him that the "white color is regarded as inherently the most perfect, not only out of custom, but this skin is the result of the free activity of blood, and the feelings that are connected with the movement of blood can present themselves through the skin" (Hegel 2007, 89). Other differences, such as hair and the shape of the skull, are also physiological (Hegel 2007, 89).

At this juncture Hegel made the connection between biological and cultural, or what he called spiritual, differences: "When racial differences are considered in such a way, they are not only external, but are essentially connected with the spiritual" (Hegel 2007, 90). In this light he considered America to be an especially interesting continent "by virtue of the fact that Europeans have settled there." It is a "mature, but also weak culture of its type. In the history of states, occupations of people are important," but because in America there were no "shepherds, no patriarchal way of life, and also no agrarian peoples, the superiority of the Europeans crushed those who were incapable of adjusting to it; when the native Americans came into contact with the European atmosphere, they were crushed by it—even when they were treated leniently" (Hegel 2007, 90). He went further in *Lectures on the Philosophy of World History* to offer a justification for what he recognized was a genocide of the indigenous populations that resulted in "nearly seven million people [being] wiped out," including the inhabitants of the West Indian islands (Hegel 1975, 163). Thus, it is that "culturally inferior nations such as these are gradually eroded through contact with more advanced nations which have gone through a more intensive cultural development" (Hegel 1975, 163).

As Teshale Tibebu, referring to the same passages quoted above, pointed out, here is Hegel exposed as the

> Christian-bourgeois philosopher at his most callous, cruel, unfeeling, and inhumane. For Hegel, the extermination of the Native Americans was necessary because it impelled a lower cultural life to give way to a higher one. Hegel reads the death toll caused by disease, war, and hard labor as a vindication of the victory of a superior culture over an inferior one, a superior race over an inferior race. What Hegel says about Native Americans is the same as what Hitler said of the so-called inferior peoples, first and foremost the Jews. For Hegel, might is right. Those who win are right, and those who lose are wrong. The victors prove their superiority over the vanquished, and the vanquished demonstrate their inferiority. (Tibebu 2011, 142–43)

From this it followed that for Hegel only those in the South American colonies, including Mexico, who could feel the need and the urge for independence were "the *Creoles*, who are descended from a mixture of native and Spanish or Portuguese ancestors. They alone have attained a higher degree of self-awareness," and if others among them do so, it is because they are not "of pure native origin" (Hegel 1975, 164). Racism has a way of distorting one's judgment or interpretation of history. If Hegel knew anything about the history of the Spanish conquest of the indigenous Taino population of Haiti in 1492, he obviously interpreted their conquest and subsequent extermination as a vindication of the superiority of the Spanish over an inferior people, as his judgment about the native peoples of the Americas above would suggest.

As I showed in chapter 1, the Spanish conquest of the island quickly led to the reduction of its population to 6 percent of its original size in twenty-two years as a consequence of the wars of conquest, diseases, and overexploitation. Still the Tainos continued to resist and launched a revolt against the Spanish in 1516 that spread to the entire island and forced the Spanish authorities to sign a peace treaty with the rebels that recognized their freedom and ceded lands to them. In 1542, the Spanish Crown issued its *Nuevas Leyes de las Indias*, which abolished the *encomienda* system[7] and declared all "Indians" free in all respects, though Charles V would revoke it in 1545 (Enzenberger 1974, 29–30). The Tainos not only revolted against the Spanish colonialists. Equating Christianity with the colonial project to subjugate and enslave them, they rejected the missionaries' attempt to convert them. As Du Tertre, a French priest, observed in his *Histoire Générale des Antilles Habitées par les François*, the main reason that such attempts have failed among the people he referred to as "savages" is the fact that they saw the Christians as "men who came to take over their and their neighbors' lands with abject cruelty; and are only looking for gold. [And] they came to have such horror of the name Christian, that the worst insult one could offer such a man would be to call him a Christian" (Du Tertre 1667, 2:414–15, bracket added).

Insofar as Hegel believed the Native Americans to be inferior to Europeans, he considered Africans still lower yet on the scale of humanity, as Mbembe pointed out. Africans, Hegel argues in *Lectures on the Philosophy of Spirit 1827–28*,

> retain a pure inwardness that never proceeds to development. The Africans are now as they have been for the last thousand years. They have never gone out of themselves, but always remain within themselves in a child manner. They have remained in the condition of raw particularity, of individuality, of desire and have not developed the oppositions of the understanding, of universal law and particular instances. They are accustomed to slavery, for freedom can exist only where the human being is conscious of himself as a universal end in itself, and reflectively knows himself as a thinking person. (Hegel 2007, 91)

In a footnote to the above passage, Robert Williams, who translated the *1827–28 Lectures*, read Hegel's last sentence above as saying that "where the human being thinks: for consciousness of freedom is the consciousness of a universality that exists in and for itself. Thus, the African, who exists in his compact, solid singularity, never comes out of this singularity (desire) and never passes over into universal life, and consequently, has no concept of right, law, state, science, and no concept of an objective God" (Hegel 2007, 91n48). In other words, for Hegel, the African who

> has not reached an awareness of any substantial subjectivity has not progressed beyond his immediate existence. As soon as man emerges as a human being, he stands in opposition to nature, and it is this alone that makes him a human being. But if he has merely made a distinction between himself and nature, he is still at the first stage of his development: he is dominated by passion and is nothing more than a savage. All our observations of African man show him to be living in a state of savagery and barbarism, and he remains in this state to the present day. (Hegel 1975, 177; also cited in Tibebu 2011, 178–79)

Tibebu put it plainly: Hegel reserved "a special place for Africans. He announces that the African does not belong to the camp of humanity proper. Here we are at the heart of Hegel's dehumanization of Africans" (2011, 179). As Lucius Outlaw also pointed out, this view of Africa "so poignantly expressed by Hegel" and shared by many others "served to validate the worst characterization as the European *invention* of Africa as a different black other to substantially rationalize and legitimate European racism and imperialism in Africa" (Outlaw 1990, 230). But Hegel's racism was not only to rationalize and legitimize European racism and imperialism in Africa. It was also to justify his argument that, as bad as it may be for the Africans who are enslaved by Europeans in America,

> their lot in their own land is even worse, since there a slavery quite as absolute exists; for it is the essential principle of slavery, that man has not yet attained a consciousness of his freedom, and consequently sinks down to a mere Thing—an object of no value. Among the Negroes moral sentiments are quite weak, or more strictly speaking, non-existent.
>
> The doctrine which we deduce from this condition of slavery among the Negroes is that which we deduce from the Idea: viz, that the "Natural condition" itself is one of absolute and thorough injustice—contravention of the Right and Just. Every intermediate grade between this and the realization of a rational State retains—as might be expected—elements and aspects of injustice. But thus existing in a State, slavery is itself a phase of advance from the mere isolated sensual existence—a phase of education—a mode of becoming

participant in a higher morality and the culture connected with it. Slavery is in and for itself *injustice*, for the essence of humanity is *Freedom*; but for this man must be matured. The gradual abolition of slavery is therefore wiser and more equitable than its sudden removal. (Hegel 1956, 96–99, emphasis in original)

Those who are inclined to believe that Hegel derived his theory of the master-slave relationship from the Saint-Domingue/Haitian Revolution must explain how, having been depicted by Hegel as not belonging to the "camp of humanity" as Tibebu pointed out, he could have seen the African slave as the subject of his celebrated thesis of the "life-and-death" struggle for recognition, or that such a slave could be capable of or willing to risk his/her life by revolting against his/her master. This is especially so since, as Hegel said, Africans were not mature enough to understand that slavery was an injustice and thus their enslavement in the American colonies was a means to *gradually* bring them out of their infancy, their sensual existence, and their savagery, and enlighten them with Christian, white European cultural principles. As Frantz Fanon put it so clearly, Hegel's view of black people is simply that they are elevated above their jungle status to the extent that they adopt European, that is, white cultural values (Fanon 1967, 18). Having thus excluded black people from being mature enough to understand the meaning of freedom and to struggle for it, I now turn to an examination of Hegel's allegory of the master-slave, or lordship and bondage relationship as he presented it in the *Phenomenology of Mind*.

HEGEL ON THE MASTER-SLAVE DIALECTIC: A CRITIQUE

In chapter 1, I showed that Marx started from the abstract conception of capitalism as necessitating the production of surplus value in the process of production. From there, he went on to reconstruct how it developed historically, thereby avoiding the trap of empiricism that starts with the concrete to arrive at the abstract formulation of the concept. To illustrate the point, the classic figure of surplus-value production is the wage-laborer who, in the process of producing commodities, creates more value than the value he/she received in the form of wages. Similarly, Marx argues, although the slave did not receive a wage, he/she nonetheless produced commodities to be sold on the world market whose values were higher than the costs of buying and maintaining that slave (see chapter 1). In other words, the concept of surplus value as the *sine qua non* of capitalism can account for both the wage-laborer and the slave in the context of the capitalist world economy since the six-teenth century.

Such is not the case for Hegel's concept of the master-slave relation, which, I will show, cannot account for the real, actual master-slave relations in Saint-Domingue (or in the Caribbean/American colonies generally). In the *Phenomenology* Hegel sought to solve the problem of recognition, which had a dual aspect or a double meaning. On the one hand, self-consciousness is possible not only in terms of the individual knowing that he/she is a person, an "I" (ego) that exists for itself, but also that it is, must be, recognized by another. The one, self-consciousness and the recognition of one's self as such, is not possible without recognition by another self-consciousness. As Hegel put it, "This process of self-consciousness in relation to another self-consciousness has in this manner been represented as the action of one alone. But this action on the part of one has itself the double significance of being at once its own action and the action of that other as well. The process [of recognition] then is absolutely the double process of both self-conscious-nesses" (Hegel 1967, 230).

For Hegel, then, self-consciousness, and the recognition of one's self as an independent person, is, by definition, a social process that results from one's interaction with others in society: "*Consciousness* finds that it immedi-ately is and is not another consciousness, as also that this other is for itself only when it cancels itself as existing for itself, and has self-existence only in the self-existence of the other" (Hegel 1967, 231, emphasis in original). At the same time, for the individual self, its existence is for itself, not for another, whom it sees as an "unessential object, as object with the impress and character of negation," and vice versa for the other. The individual self-consciousness, in short, "makes its appearance in antithesis to another" (Heg-el 1967, 231).

Each individual may be certain of its self as self, but not of the other, which thus makes the individual doubt the truth of its own self. For that not to happen, the individual must be able to prove to itself that it exists as an independent object, that "it is fettered to no determinate existence, that it is not bound at all by the particularity everywhere characteristic of existence as such, and is *not* tied up with life" (Hegel 1967, 232, emphasis in original). This process of self-certain existence brings about action on the part of both individuals in such a way that "in so far as it is the other's action, each aims at the destruction and death of the other. But in this there is implicated also the second kind of action, self-activity; for the former implies that it risks its own life. The relation of both self-consciousnesses is in this way so consti-tuted that they prove themselves and each other through a life-and-death struggle" (Hegel 1967, 232). To achieve this certainty of their self-existence, of being for themselves, however, each individual must be willing to risk its life, for "it is solely by risking life that freedom is obtained" (Hegel 1967, 233). The individual who has not staked or refuses to stake his/her life may "be recognized as a Person; but he has not attained the truth of this recogni-tion as an independent self-consciousness" (Hegel 1967, 233).

At the same time, the two individuals engaged in this life-and-death strug-gle have risked their lives, but they cannot annihilate each other since that would deny each of them the certainty of self-existence: "death is the natural 'negation' of consciousness" (Hegel 1967, 233). This realization leads the parties to "sublate" their "terms of extremes seeking to have existence on their own account" (Hegel 1967, 233). This awareness that "*life* is as essen-tial to it as pure-self-consciousness" (Hegel 1967, 234), leads to the under-standing of what Alexandre Kojève explained as the necessity for the human individual to transcend his/her "animal Desire"—that is, Desire existing purely for itself—by recognizing that human Desire can only be social, that human existence is possible only insofar as the "Desire of each member of the herd must be directed—or potentially directed—toward the Desires of the other members. If human reality is social reality, society is human only as a set of Desires mutually desiring one another as Desires" (Kojève 1969, 6). This sociality produces a free individual "conscious of his individuality, his freedom, his history, and finally, his historicity" (Kojève 1969, 6).

On this social or anthropogenic basis, "self-consciousness becomes aware that *life* is as essential to it as pure self-consciousness" (Hegel 1967, 234). There are, then, two moments in the development of self-consciousness. In the first moment, consciousness is immediate consciousness wherein ego sees itself as an absolute object independent of all others. In the second moment, that conception of absolute independence is dissolved and gives rise to consciousness not as purely for itself, but for another as well, that is, "an existent consciousness, consciousness in the form and shape of thinghood" (Hegel 1967, 234). In other words, in the struggle to the death for recognition between these two self-consciousnesses, they stand opposed to one another as two "forms or modes of consciousnesses. The one is independent, and its essential nature is to be for itself; the other is dependent, and its essence is life or existence for another. The former is the Master, or Lord, the latter the Bondsman" or slave (Hegel 1967, 234).

Given that, as a result of this struggle, the one who became master by demonstrating that he was willing to risk his life, which he considered "to be merely something negative," had the power to hold the bondsman/slave in subordination (Hegel 1967, 235). The bondsman/slave, who has been reduced to "thinghood" by the master, rejects that reduction and struggles against it. But unable to go so far as to "annihilate it outright and be done with it he merely works on it" (Hegel 1967, 235). In this dual process, the master "gets his recognition through another consciousness, for in them the latter affirms itself as unessential, both by working on the thing, and, on the other hand, by the fact of being dependent on a determinate existence." On this basis, "a form of recognition has arisen that is one sided and unequal" (Hegel 1967, 236).

But if, for the master, the "unessential consciousness" of the bondsman/slave is the "truth of his certainty of himself," it is also the case that "this object does not correspond to its notion." By this Hegel meant that just at the moment when the master believed he had achieved his independent consciousness, it was in fact the opposite that happened, namely, that the master's is in reality a dependent consciousness. The master finds, in other words, that the "truth of the independent consciousness is the consciousness of the bondsman. [J]ust as lordship showed its essential nature to be the reverse of what it wants to be, so, too, bondage will, when completed, pass into the opposite of what it immediately is: being a consciousness repressed within itself, it will enter into itself, and change round into real and true independence" (Hegel 1967, 237).

Up to now, Hegel argues, we had believed that self-consciousness existed for the master only because he was thought to be the "essential reality for the state of bondage," an "independent existence existing for itself." But the bondsman/slave also contains this "truth of pure negativity and self-existence because it has experienced this reality within it" (Hegel 1967, 238). The slave, who recognized the master's self-consciousness and autonomy, also values the reality and autonomy of human freedom, but is not able to realize that objective for him-/herself and is not recognized by the master. The slave, who feared death and the sovereign master, dissolves his/her dependence and subordination to the master and attains self-consciousness: "through work and labor this consciousness of the bondsman comes to itself." If for the master the "thing seemed to fall to the lot of the servant [and] [d]esire reserved to itself the pure negating of the object and thereby unalloyed feeling of self," labor is "what shapes and fashions the thing. The negative relation to the object passes into the *form* of the object, into something that is permanent and remains; because it is just for the laborer that the object has independence" (Hegel 1967, 238).

The labor of transforming the object, however, is not the only factor that makes the slave aware of his/her self-existence; it also negates the element of fear and thereby allows the slave to become a self-existent being: "In fashioning the thing, self-existence comes to be felt explicitly as his own proper being, and he attains the consciousness that he himself exists in its own right and on its own account. Thus precisely in labor where there seemed to be merely some outsider's mind and ideas involved, the bondsman becomes aware, through his rediscovery of himself by himself, of having and being a 'mind of his own'" (Hegel 1967, 239).

In his interpretation of Hegel, Kojève argues that in this struggle for recognition, the slave would win out in the end. Because the master is unable to recognize the slave, "he is at an impasse," whereas the slave, who recognized the master but seeks recognition from him, "must impose himself on the Master and be recognized by him. To be sure, for this to take place, the Slave must cease to be a Slave: he must transcend himself, 'overcome' himself, as Slave" (Kojève 1969, 21).

It may be possible to read this as an argument for the slave to end the master-slave relationship violently, as Fisher suggests (2004, 29). But for that to happen, Kojève would need to abandon the idea that the slave can gain recognition from the master through and by labor, such that "in becoming master of Nature by work, the Slave frees himself from his own nature, from his own instinct that tied him to Nature and made him the Master's Slave. Therefore, by freeing the Slave from Nature, work frees him from himself as well, from his Slave's nature: it frees him from the Master. The future and History hence belong not to the warlike Master, who either dies or preserves himself indefinitely in identity to himself, but to the working Slave" (Kojève 1969, 23).

Unlike Kojève, I argue that, if we consider the *real* slavery in the colonies of the Americas (as opposed to the allegorical situation depicted by Hegel), the slave was not looking to gain the recognition of the master and freedom through labor. Instead, as Gordon Lewis put it, the slave revolted because, "as a person, he wanted his liberty. No doubt he hated the system. But he wanted, above all else, to get the individual instruments of that system—the master, overseer, driver—off his back" (Lewis 1983, 223). As Marx made clear, alienated labor, whether it is performed by a slave or a wage-laborer, is labor "that is not voluntary, but coerced." This is because in capitalist society workers are expropriated from the means of production and have no alternative but to sell their labor-power in return for a wage in order to live. That is why, Marx argues, for the worker labor "appears in the fact that it is not his own, but someone else's, that it does not belong to him, that in it he belongs, not to himself, but to another" (Marx 1975, 274). Alienated labor, therefore, no matter whether it is produced by a slave or a "free" wage-laborer, is unfreedom.

The point I am making here is that an individual can never be considered to be "free" and exercise self-agency as long as he/she depends on working for someone else to obtain the wherewithal to live a decent life. That is why in his 1857 "Critique of the Gotha Program," Marx argues that real human and individual freedom could not be achieved until

> the enslaving subordination of the individual to the division of labour, and therewith also the antithesis between mental and physical labour, has vanished; after labour has become not only a means of life but life's prime want; after the productive forces have also increased with the all-round development of the individual, and all the springs of co-operative wealth flow more abundantly—only then can the narrow horizon of bourgeois right be crossed in its entirety and society inscribed on its banners: from each according to his ability, to each according to his needs! (Marx 1977, 569)

Expressed differently, Marx's point is that individual agency and human freedom cannot be achieved unless and until access to the necessities of life—food, housing, clothing, transportation, health care, education, leisure, and so on—is delinked from one's labor. Labor, in other words, would no longer be the basis for the exploitation of one man/woman or one class by another or for the creation of a social division of labor whereby different groups (divided into owners/managers, skilled/unskilled, gender, ethnicity, race, nationality) occupy different and unequal positions, and the unequal distribution of wealth, income, benefits, and so forth, that follow from that. It does not follow, however, that labor would become unnecessary; it is a "means of life" and no society can survive without producing the goods and services that satisfy human needs and desires. But acquiring those goods and services would no longer be dependent on one's labor, status, income, or wealth, and their corresponding unequal consequences and quality of life. They would instead become public goods available to one and all as basic human rights. Hence, Marx's principle above that in such a decent society each individual would contribute according to his/her ability but receive what he/she needs independently of that contribution.

It is also clear that Hegel could never have come to such a conclusion about alienated labor because, as Marx pointed out, Hegel understood "the self-creation of man [*sic*] as a process, conceives objectification as loss of the object, as alienation and as transcendence of this alienation; thus, [he] grasps the essence of *labour* as the outcome of man's *own labour*." Hegel's standpoint is ultimately that of political economy because the "only labour which Hegel knows and recognizes is *abstractly mental* labour," not the real, alienated labor that results from the exploitation of the laborer by the capitalist (Marx 1975, 332–33, emphasis in original). Nowhere is this made clearer than in Hegel's analysis of the lord-bondsman/master-slave dialectic in the *Phenomenology*.

Unlike Kojève's reading, then, my view of Hegel accords with that of Adeleke Adeeko, who argues that just because the master "is fulfilling a desire should not be construed as saying that the slave lacks the capacity to exercise subjective will" (Adeeko 2005, 19). By this he meant that in slavery, "the subjected person continues to seek an opportunity to exercise the will to 'die,' or, to say the same thing, to be free," not only from the master but from having to labor for another's benefit. In all slave societies, he suggests, and as Lewis pointed out above, masters were in constant fear of rebellions "because the slave's wish to literally die conflicts with the master's desire to live and to prevent the slave from exercising his death wish." Thus, the fact that slavery caused slave rebellion is "a phenomenological truth that Hegel did not analyze in Lordship and Bondage" (Adeeko 2005, 19). In short, it is not through labor that the slave frees him-/herself; he/she does so by being willing to risk his/her life, to revolt, "to negate the master literally and not just intellectually" to achieve that freedom (Adeeko 2005, 18). The reason Hegel could not have considered that phenomenological truth for *real* slaves, African slaves in the colonies in particular, then, is because for him, as previously noted, the African, who never "made the distinction between himself and nature" remained at "the first stage of his development," and was "nothing more than a savage living in a state of savagery and barbarism." Or, to use Kojève's analogy, for Hegel, the African slave "never went beyond the stage of animal desire."

The slaves of Saint-Domingue did not encounter their masters until they were brought there from Africa, where they had been captured by other Africans working on behalf of powerful African rulers and wealthy merchants who profited from the slave trade; chained and shackled with heavy stones to prevent them from escaping; and transported to the ports to be sold to European traders (Portuguese, Dutch, English, French) and embarked on the slave ships for the transatlantic crossing to be sold to plantation owners in the Americas (Blackburn 2011; Curtin 1975; Thornton 1998). On the ships, they were separated by gender, packed in the hold for the duration of the passage, during which they endured the most horrible human conditions possible (Behrendt, Eltis, and Richardson 2001, 455; De Vaissière 1909; James 1963, 7–8). But, not knowing, as Hegel postulated, that they were not mature enough to understand the meaning of freedom and that not risking their lives and accepting their servitude was their way out of their "state of barbarism," they, as did their Taino predecessors, rebelled against their cruel and inhumane treatment.

As C. L. R. James pointed out, "contrary to the lies that have been spread about Negro docility, the revolts were incessant, so that the slaves had to be chained and attached in rows to long iron bars" to stifle them (James 1963, 8). Pierre de Vaissière also showed that the revolts were frequent and took different forms. Some were passive, when, for example, the slaves refused to eat, choosing death over enslavement. To deter such acts, ship captains would sometimes have the slaves' arms and legs cut off, and worse cruelties yet awaited those who took up arms against the ship's crews (de Vaissière 1909, 161–62). Other revolts were violent. According to Stephen Behrendt, David Eltis, and David Richardson, between 1698 and 1807, there were at least 388 cases of slave revolts aboard slave ships destined for the Americas. Most of those revolts were suppressed, but some slaves succeeded in freeing themselves and returning to Africa. In total, nearly 10 percent of all slave ships experienced revolts, and of the approximately 6.6 million slaves who were taken from Africa and brought to the Americas between 1680 and 1800, slave revolts and resistance resulted in 600,000, or nearly 10 percent, fewer slaves reaching their destinations while adding also to the costs of transporting the remainders to the Americas (Behrendt, Eltis, and Richardson 2001, 455, 463, 473).

Once on the plantations, however, the slaves would be subjected to more cruelty and violence. They would be branded with a hot iron with the initials or particular mark of their masters. To constrain their movements, intimidate, and instill fear in them, the slaves were often forced to wear iron collars around their necks or chains around their hands and feet, or to drag wooden blocks behind them. Masters burned their skins or their buttocks and poured hot cinders, salt, pepper, and citron on their wounds. They mutilated the slaves by pouring burning wax or cane syrup on them, pulling their teeth, or cutting them open and pouring melted lard on the cuts. They buried them up to their necks near wasps' nests, or they made the slaves eat their own excrement, burned them alive, or blew them up with gunpowder. Though most of these cruelties were meted out to men, women were not spared. As the ones who fed the canes to the mills, their hands often got caught in the rollers and their hands or arms would have to be severed lest their entire body would be crushed. In short, the slaves labored under the direct compulsion of their commanders—some of whom had been recruited among Creole slaves toward the end of the eighteenth century—whose whips would lash out at one and all, men, women, children, old or young as they saw fit to keep them in line (de Vaissière 1909, 165–68; Dupuy 1989, 33–34; Fick 1990, 35; Gisler 1965, 62, 73; James 1963, 12–13).

This summary of the master's attitude toward and relation to the slave was to make the point that, contrary to Hegel, the master in Saint-Domingue saw the slave as a mere instrument of labor, a "body of extraction" as Mbembe pointed out previously, and as such was not in the least interested in being recognized and respected by him/her. Moreover, as I have shown, the slave system of the Americas was a system of *racial* slavery, not the color-less and sanitized one Hegel depicted in the *Phenomenology*. It is therefore not possible to separate the barbarity of this system, its total dehumanization of the slave, from the fact that the white masters of Europe were dealing first and foremost with black slaves they considered to be less than fully human, as did Hegel. This is what led Fanon to argue that the slave master in the Caribbean "differs from the master described by Hegel. For Hegel there is reciprocity; here the master laughs at the consciousness of the slave. What he wants from the slave is not recognition but work" (Fanon 1967, 220n8).[8] Sidney Mintz made the same point: "Slaves were not *primarily* a source of prestige, or sexual gratification, of the satisfaction of sadistic impulses, or anything else but profit—and of profit within a frankly capitalistic system" (Mintz 1974, 47).

This point is worth emphasizing. As I pointed out also in the previous chapter, the system of racial slavery in the Americas was a thoroughly capi-talist enterprise established for the sole purpose of producing wealth for the colonial powers and for the planter classes. Whether it was in the production of sugar, cotton, or coffee, the slaves were exploited to the maximum extent possible. As long as the supply of slaves remained relatively constant and the prices the masters paid for them relatively low, the planters worked their slaves to the point of exhaustion and death; and since the birthrate was always lower than the death rate among slaves, due in part also to the refusal of women slaves to carry their pregnancies to term so as not to breed new slaves (Neptune Anglade 1986, 94), the slave population could be replenished only by constantly importing more slaves from Africa.

It should come as no surprise, then, that, as Antoine Métral observed in his *Histoire de l'insurrection des esclaves dans le Nord de Saint-Domingue*, of all the causes of the uprising of the slaves in Saint-Domingue in August 1791, the most important "is the love of liberty that exists among all men. The more horrible the servitude, the stronger is the love of liberty. The furors of liberty blended with those of servitude" (Métral 1818, 9, 11). Long before the insurrection in 1791, there had been many other revolts and maroon raids on plantations in the colony (in 1522, 1679, 1691, 1723, 1747, 1757) whose explicit objectives were to kill all the whites, and, in the case of the revolt by Makandal in 1757, the first one organized with the explicit objective of declaring the colony's independence (Dupuy 1989, 34; Fick 1990, 62; James 1963, 20–22; Midy 2009, 133).

Franklin Midy, making a point similar to Adeeko's, summarized the issue clearly. There was no time when the colonial authorities were not fully conscious of the fact that the slave colonies "sheltered an 'internal enemy' that could be protected only by a constantly active system of dehumanization, surveillance, and repression. Any time such a system becomes deactivated or inoperative, it releases the long-suppressed massive human energy" (2009, 144). As Gordon Lewis also put it,

> slave insurrectionism—accompanied, of course, by the history of uprising on slave ships—confers upon Caribbean history two cardinal elements: one is that of historical magnitude, for the slave masses, in their successive revolts— starting, perhaps, with the slave insurrection in Santo Domingo in 1522— demonstrated that they could storm the heights of heaven in a way that not even Marx fully appreciated; and the other is that of historical continuity, in the sense that every revolt before 1791 in Saint-Domingue led up to, and prepared the way for, that grand finale, while every revolt after 1791 was influenced by its tremendous success. (Lewis 1983, 224)

There is no question that the French Revolution of 1789 and its ideals of liberty and equality for all also played a key role in moving the slaves to act and take matters into their own hands with the support and encouragement of their allies among the free Creole population, mulatto and black. When placed in the context of the long history of resistance, maroon raids, and revolts by the slaves of Saint-Domingue—and elsewhere in the Caribbean, such as for example, the rebellions in St. John in 1733, Antigua in 1736, Jamaica in 1760, and Berbice in 1763–1764 (Thompson 1998, 77)—before 1791, the Saint-Domingue Revolution was not only *thinkable*, but also, as Vertus Saint-Louis put it, "possible and *predictable*" (Saint-Louis 2008, 164, emphasis in original).

My view here, therefore, differs from that of Michel-Rolph Trouillot, who argues that "the Haitian Revolution entered history with the peculiar characteristic of being unthinkable as it happened." Those reading about the revolution in France from 1790 to 1804, he contended, were incapable of understanding the "ongoing Revolution in its own terms. They could read the news only with their ready-made categories, and these categories were incompatible with the idea of a slave revolution." Moreover, for him the "key issue is not ideological. The issue is rather epistemological and, by inference, methodological in the broadest sense" (Trouillot 1991, 82). This is because as Europe was engaged in its colonial conquests and killing and enslaving other human beings since the sixteenth century, and European philosophers, politicians, theologians, and artists were contemplating the meaning of "Man," it was agreed that he "was of European ancestry and male." And the "Enlightenment did not remove the fundamental ambiguity that dominated the encounter between ontological discourse and colonial practice" (Trouillot 1991, 83; also in Trouillot 1995, ch. 3).

Trouillot goes even further by arguing that the revolution was not only unthinkable and unannounced in the West, but also, and "to a large extent unspoken among the slaves themselves," by which he meant that it was not "accompanied by an explicit intellectual discourse." This was not only because most slaves were "illiterate and that the printed word was not a realistic means of propaganda in the context of a slave colony. But another reason was that the claims of the revolution were indeed too radical to be formulated in advance of its deeds. Victorious practice could assert them only *after the fact*. In that sense, the revolution was indeed at the limits of the thinkable, even in Saint-Domingue, even among the slaves themselves, even among its own leaders" (Trouillot 1991, 88, emphasis in original).

I agree with Trouillot's assertion about the undeniable association between European colonial conquests and the development of racist ideologies of western European/white (and male) supremacy, of which Hegel was a prototype. That is why I have argued above that he could not have taken the *real* slave of Saint-Domingue as his representative for the master-slave dialectic. It does not follow, however, that there existed or could ever be one and only one ontology or worldview in western Europe (or among any other group or culture) to the exclusion of all others. As Dale Tomich points out, Trouillot considers western Europeans as having a "singular ontology of social being [that] determines the general historic content of European thought with regard to non-Western peoples." Consequently, he "interprets the Western ontology as a distinct, independent, and enduring structure—internally unified, externally closed and bounded—that regulates thinkability by processes of inclusion and exclusion. [T]here is only one voice that speaks for Western domination and colonial practice. The field is arbitrarily divided between insiders who understand and outsiders who do not (and cannot) understand" (Tomich 2008, 406–7).

Trouillot applied this same singular, exclusionary perspective to his understanding of the Saint-Domingue/Haitian Revolution. In a similar vein as Tomich, Carlo Célius observed that Trouillot portrayed "the Haitian Revolution as a self-enclosed entity that unfurled on its own, completely impermeable to all 'exogenous' relations. Can we really detach the Haitian Revolution from the context of the French Revolution?" he asked. And is it necessary to "deny its links to the latter in order to clarify the specificity of the former? The relations that exist between both revolutions take nothing away from the specific characteristics of [either] one of them. The problem is to determine the nature and the significance of these relations. Michel-Rolph Trouillot simply denies them" (Célius 1997, 13). Tomich also remarked poignantly that the "Haitian and French Revolutions influenced one another because they were related. They were not related because they influenced one another. The ideas of the Enlightenment and the French Revolution did not travel to Haiti to exert their influence. Ideas, movements and institutions reverberated across the Atlantic and interacted with one another because they were part of the same complex of transatlantic relations" (Tomich 2008, 413).

But Saint-Domingue was also an integral and major part of the Atlantic world in the eighteenth century, where not only goods, commodities, and people of all shades but ideas, news, and information moved to and from the French colony and the other territories, colonies, and independent states of the Americas, such as the United States. And just as with the French Revolution, so it was with its predecessor in the United States where it had even greater resonance and implications. As Ronald Johnson argued, the majority of the American public may have opposed the 1791 uprising in Saint-Domingue but many also

> overcame their racialized views of the diaspora to see revolutionary images from Saint-Domingue as not dissimilar to those that played out on mainland soil in the 1770s. African cries of "liberty or death" penetrated inflexible racial barriers in U.S. society. The readiness of formerly enslaved people to mete out violent resistance and to sacrifice their lives for freedom garnered a measured level of understanding from a nation born out of the same radical stimulus. (Johnson 2014, 10)

The 1791 uprising proved to be the decisive event that put an end to the master-slave relations, if not to other forms of class domination that would emerge during the revolution and after Haiti became independent. The radicalness of the revolution of Saint-Domingue, however, was that the slaves were fighting not only to get rid of their masters but to free themselves from having to labor for anyone else as a *conditio sine qua non* of their own existence. Contrary to Trouillot's assertion, therefore, the slaves of Saint-Domingue did not need to have issued a manifesto to announce their upcoming uprising and their objectives. They had already "written" that manifesto in their actions prior to 1791, and, in some cases like the Makandal revolt of 1757, their explicit objective to destroy the slave regime and create a different social order whose subsequent development, like those of any revolution that came before or after, would be determined by concrete, unforeseen, and unpredictable conditions, contradictions, and struggles that no a priori blueprint could anticipate.

As I will show in the next chapter, after Toussaint Louverture took control of the colony in 1800, and in keeping with the reforms proposed earlier by the French commissioners Etienne Polverel and Léger Félicité Sonthonax, he opposed the breakup of the plantations and sought to revitalize the production of sugar and other commodities for export (coffee, cotton, indigo) that had made Saint-Domingue the wealthiest Caribbean colony in the eighteenth century. To accomplish that objective, Louverture sought to compel the former slaves to return to their old plantations and keep them there under harsh discipline. The main difference between this and the old system was that now the former slaves would be paid wages and/or a share of the products and given access to small plots on the margins of the plantations they could cultivate for themselves, as was the practice under slavery.

But the slaves fought against that alternative as well. They fled to the mountains and disrupted production by looting and burning the plantations, and they rebelled against Toussaint's government (Repussard 1802; also cited in Dupuy 1989, 64–66). So severe was the labor shortage that Toussaint's government contemplated making plans with the English and Americans to import slaves from Africa, intending to free them once they arrived, but obligating them to work for the planters who paid for them (Ardouin 1958, 4:77; Fick 1990, 209; Lacroix 1820, 2:58; also cited in Dupuy 1989, 24). The objective of the former slaves was to control their own labor and the fruits of that labor, or, put differently, to end their exploitation by slave masters or by buyers of labor-power. Carolyn Fick, referring to an argument offered by a colonial observer, summarized the attitude of the former slaves succinctly: they were simply opposed to the reimposition of production for profit and of capitalist competition, "in short, the virtues of Western capitalist ethic" (Fick 1990, 179).

In an assessment of Fanon's reading of Hegel's master-slave dialectic, Anthony Bogues offered a similar conclusion: "The master wants the slave to work and desires recognition only to the extent that it will make the slave work. The slave wants freedom and faces the master to destroy the system of slavery. This is a new dialectic, neither one of recognition nor one of unequal encounter, but one in which new forms of freedom are being imagined, plotted, and enacted wherever possible" (Bogues 2010, 114). It must be pointed out, however, that as radical as the objectives of the slave were, they were not rejecting the concept of property ownership as such. That is, they were not calling for common ownership of property and an egalitarian redistribution of the goods to be produced in the new society they envisioned. Their aim, rather, was to become owners or possessors of their own property to produce and consume what they needed for themselves and their families as well as exchange surpluses in a market, but one that they controlled. In short, the objective of the slaves was to transform themselves into what Sidney Mintz called a "reconstituted peasantry" to create an alternative way of life that reflected their most immediate interests: the desire for land and self-sufficiency (Mintz 1974, 132–33; Dupuy 1989, 56). To borrow a phrase from Mbembe (who was speaking about the desire of the enslaved in general), they fought to reconstitute themselves as a "*body*, to produce themselves as a free and sovereign community, ideally through their own work and achievements. They sought to make themselves their own points of origin, their own certainty, and their own destination in the world" (Mbembe 2017, 33–34).

The struggles between the new ruling class brought into being by Toussaint Louverture's regime and the former slaves would continue before and after Haiti became independent in 1804 and lead to what I have called a Pyrrhic victory for the laboring classes and the stalemate of the bourgeoisie. By this I meant that, on the one hand, the new bourgeoisie was unable to proletarianize the former slaves or their descendants because they succeeded in gaining access to land, whether or not they had legal property titles, or as sharecroppers. On the other hand, not having gained control of the state and its apparatuses of dominance, the former slaves could not prevent the dominant classes from instituting new forms of domination and exploitation. Unable to exploit the former slaves directly from the process of production, the new bourgeoisie accumulated its wealth from the rents they imposed on the tenant farmers or sharecroppers (i.e., those without access to land of their own), by controlling the prices they paid to the farmers for their crops, by taxing their products, and by reselling on the domestic market the commodities they imported from abroad. But this also meant that the new bourgeoisie was essentially limited to accumulating wealth primarily from the circulation rather than the production process (except in the case of the sharecroppers), a fact that made it difficult to lay the conditions for the creation of an integrated domestic market and the development of national industries in the nineteenth century (see Dupuy 1989, chs. 3–4; 2014, ch. 3).

It is clear to me from the arguments I have offered here that Hegel could not have derived his master-slave dialectic from the Saint-Domingue Revolution as Buck-Morss, Tavares, and Nesbitt contend, because the abstract concept he outlined in the *Phenomenology of Mind* cannot account for or explain the concrete and its many determinations that were manifested and crystallized in Saint-Domingue. Those who became masters in Saint-Domingue were not looking to be recognized by their slaves, but were interested only in their labor to extract the maximum surplus from them in the shortest time possible. For their part, the Africans who became the slaves of Saint-Domingue, and those who were born in the colony (hence the difference made between *bosal* and *Kreyòl/Creole* slaves, respectively, at the time of the revolution), were not afraid to risk their lives to win their freedom when they were captured and transported to Saint-Domingue, or after they were confined to their plantations. And neither did they seek to gain recognition from their masters through their labor. Instead they fought for and succeeded in freeing themselves from having to labor for their masters by getting rid of them by violent means. They also envisioned an alternative world in which they would be masters of their own labor and of their own lives, but one that also contained its own contradictions and limitations. Blinded as he was by his racism, Hegel could never have understood that fundamental ontological truth.

NOTES

1. See, for example, Orlando Patterson, *Slavery and Social Death: A Comparative Study* (1982); Frantz Fanon, *Black Skin, White Masks* (1967); David Brion Davis, *The Problem of Slavery in the Age of Revolution, 1770–1823* (1975); Paul Gilroy, *The Black Atlantic: Modernity and Double Consciousness* (1995); Adeleke Adeeko, *The Slave's Rebellion: Literature, History, Orature* (2005); and Teshale Tibebu, *Hegel and the Third World: The Making of Eurocentrism in World History* (2011).

2. According to Albert Soboul, Jean-Baptiste Carrier had been sent by the National Convention along with others to suppress the counterrevolution in the provinces, where, as the representative on mission in Nantes, he allowed the executions of thousands of people by drowning without trial. Considered to be a terrorist, he would be denounced in 1794 by the Committee of Public Safety, brought to trial before the Revolutionary Tribunal, and executed on December 16, 1794 (1989, 342, 384, 426).

3. J. M. Petry, the editor and translator of Hegel's *Philosophy of Subjective Spirit*, cited Baubrun Ardoin's *Études sur l'Histoire d'Haiti*, Vol. 4, 358 (published in 1853/60) as a source, which Hegel could not possibly have used because he died in 1831. More plausible is another publication Petry cited: L. Dubroca, *La Vie de Toussaint-Louverture* published in Paris in 1802.

4. Kate Ramsey calls attention to the fact that in "Haiti the word Vodou has traditionally referred to a particular mode of dance and drumming, and has generally not been figured as an inclusive term for the entire range of spiritual and healing practices undertaken within extended families and through relationships with male and female religious leaders, called, respectively, *oungan* and *manbo*. . . . For many practitioners, the encompassing term is not Vodou, but rather Ginen, a powerful moral philosophy and ethical code valorizing ancestral African ways of serving spirits and living in the world" (Ramsey 2011, 7, emphasis in original).

5. For a succinct analysis of the ideological formulations and how they were used to mask the class interests of the dominant classes under and since Toussaint Louverture, see Michel-Rolph Trouillot's *Ti Difé Boulé sou istoua ayiti* (1977, 195–209).

6. See also the discussion of Louverture's objectives in chapter 3.

7. The *encomienda* system introduced by the Spanish throughout their territories in the Americas consisted of allocating the conquered population to an *encomendero* depending on his rank and importance in the colony. The higher the rank and influence, the more Tainos one received (Las Casas 1974, 52). In effect, the Tainos became the slaves of the *encomendero*.

8. By "here" Fanon meant the French Caribbean colonies of Martinique and Guadeloupe, not Saint-Domingue.

Chapter Three

From Saint-Domingue to Haiti

Revolution and the Rise of a New Bourgeoisie

A revolution, Perry Anderson suggested, is "the political overthrow from below of one state order, and its replacement by another. It is an episode of convulsive political transformation, compressed in time and concentrated in target, that has a determinate beginning—when the old state apparatus is intact—and a definite end, when that apparatus is decisively broken and a new one erected in its stead" (Anderson 1984, 112).

As I argue below, the slave uprising in Saint-Domingue in August 1791 turned into a full-blown revolution that led to the dismantling of the old colonial state apparatus and replacing it with a new one when Haiti declared its independence in 1804. To be more precise, the new state apparatus began to be constructed in 1800 when Toussaint Louverture and his revolutionary forces took control of the colony. Thus, the period between 1800 and 1804 may be seen as one of transition during which the class and political structures of the new state were being constructed.

By all measures the Haitian Revolution of 1791–1804 was the most radical of all eighteenth-century revolutions and an epochal event. The American Revolution of 1776 and the French Revolution of 1789 fought for the principles of national self-determination, liberty, equality, and fraternity, but limited them to European and white American men only. And both of these preceding revolutions sought to maintain the system of chattel slavery and its attendant racial stratification order by declaring that black men and women were not fully human and hence were unqualified for citizenship, equality, liberty, and self-rule. The Haitian Revolution, fought by men and women slaves and free peoples of color, but led by men, challenged the premises of the colonial, slave, and white supremacy systems, and declared once and for all that the ideals of liberty, equality, justice, and self-determination championed by the two previous revolutions and embodied in the philosophies of the Enlightenment belonged to all of humanity and not only to those segments of it privileged by skin color or social position.

The impact of the Haitian Revolution also went far beyond the borders of the French colony of Saint-Domingue, which was given its aboriginal Taino name of Haiti after it declared its independence on January 1, 1804. The revolutionary forces not only defeated the armies of France, England, and Spain in their war of independence, but also destroyed the wealthiest planter class and Caribbean colony of the New World. The 455,000 slaves of Saint-Domingue, which was slightly larger in area than the state of Maryland, outproduced all the English Caribbean and French sugar colonies put together and supplied about half of the sugar and coffee consumed in Europe and the Americas at the time of the French Revolution of 1789 (Williams 1970, 238–39; Geggus 2002, 5). Born in that part of the world where colonialism and slavery still dominated, the victory of the black slaves and free people of color of Saint-Domingue sent shock waves throughout Europe and the Americas. Slaveholders everywhere feared that the spirit of rebellion would spread among their own slaves and took measures to restrict immigration from Saint-Domingue. The newly formed Republic of Haiti also provided direct assistance to the struggle for independence and the abolition of slavery in Venezuela in 1820, and Haiti's intervention in 1822 in Spanish Santo Domingo, with which Haiti shared the island of Hispaniola, led to the abolition of slavery there as well (Geggus 2002, 27–28; Moya Pons 1998, 122–24).

Since 1804 the revolution also stood as the symbol of black freedom from slavery, racism, and colonial oppression everywhere. In his speech in Haiti on January 1, 2004, to commemorate the bicentenary of the revolution, South African president Thabo Mbeki stated that the Haitian Revolution must be celebrated "because it dealt a deadly blow to the slave traders who had scoured the coasts of West and East Africa for slaves and ruined the lives of millions of Africans," and because of "the heroic deeds of these Africans who single-mindedly struggled for their freedom and inspired many of us to understand that none but ourselves can defeat those who subject us to tyranny, oppression and exploitation" (Mbeki 2004). Randall Robinson, founder and former president of TransAfrica, wrote, "The revolution was fought by

Haitians but won for all of us. The blacks of St. Domingue forced the world to see both them and the millions of other Africans enslaved throughout the Americas with new eyes. They had banished slavery from their land and proclaimed it an official refuge for escaped slaves from anywhere in the world. They had shattered the myth of European invincibility" (Robinson 2004).

And C. L. R. James, author of *The Black Jacobins: Toussaint Louverture and the San Domingo Revolution*, which in my view still remains the classic interpretation of the revolution, put it thusly: "The revolt is the only successful slave revolt in history, and the odds it had to overcome is evidence of the magnitude of the interests that were involved. The transformation of slaves, trembling in hundreds before a single white man, into a people able to organise themselves and defeat the most powerful European nations of their day, is one of the great epics of revolutionary struggle and achievement" (James 1963, ix).

Yet if the Haitian Revolution stood for so much, it must also be recognized, as Ada Ferrer notes, that it had a limited impact on slave emancipation in the rest of the hemisphere, notwithstanding the fear of slave uprisings among planters and colonial governments in the region. Not only did Bonaparte restore slavery in Martinique and Guadeloupe, but the slave trade continued to thrive. Despite growing anti-slavery sentiments in England, three-quarters of a million people were still enslaved in the English Caribbean colonies; and though abolitionism also grew in the northern states of the United States, slavery remained entrenched in the south where pro-slavery forces were contemplating expanding it to other parts of the country. Except for the abolition of slavery in Santo Domingo with the direct military support of Haiti, slavery continued to grow in the other Spanish Caribbean colonies of Cuba and Puerto Rico. In Cuba especially, slave owners and planters capitalized on the demise of slavery in Saint-Domingue to become the largest sugar producer and one of the largest importers of slaves in the world in the nineteenth century (Ferrer 2009, 223–25; see also chapter 1).

But if the Saint-Domingue Revolution could be said to have dealt the first major blow to this odious system of oppression and exploitation, it neither addressed nor resolved the division of society into dominant and subordinate, exploiting and exploited classes. As I will show below, although the slaves started the revolution and sought to become independent landowning farmers, those who emerged as its leaders and took control of the colonial state in 1800 had a different objective: to become the new rulers of the colony,

preserve the plantation system and production for export, become a landowning bourgeoisie, and transform the former slaves into free-wage laborers to
work on the plantations. From 1800 to 1804, a struggle emerged between
these two opposite objectives while the war between the revolutionary forces
and the French raged on until the latter were defeated and Haiti gained its
independence. It is in this sense that I argue that the slave revolution of Saint-
Domingue was transformed into a bourgeois revolution.

I will also show that the rise of this new and predominantly black bourgeoisie that comprised the leadership and high-ranking officers and functionaries of the Louverture government confronted the "free people of color"
predominantly comprising mulattoes who had been a property- and slave-
owning class before the revolution. They, too, aspired to control the colonial
state and had led an unsuccessful civil war against Louverture in 1799 (see
Dupuy 1989, 52; Fick 1990, 200–203). The conflicts between these two
factions rekindled the ideologies of racial and color divisions that served as
the bedrock of the slave order to justify their struggles to control the economy and the state and its attendant apparatuses of repression after independence.

As Micheline Labelle expressed it, what in Haiti is thought of as the
"color question" refers to none other than the "historical struggles that have
opposed the 'black' and 'mulatto' factions of the dominant classes. However,
it also implies a problematic of identity that affects the entire society, ex-
pressing in different ways and at different levels, the totality of social dis-
courses and practices" (Labelle 1978, 13). Some, Labelle argues, have considered the "color question" as secondary to the "social question," as a ploy
to manipulate the subordinate masses. By contrast, others have seen it as
fundamental to explaining the unequal distribution of wealth and privileges
to the "mulatto" minority at the expense of the "black" majority, and to
rallying the latter against the former. However, that approach overlooks the
fact that the class structure of the society comprises both of these ascribed
categories of color, and in invoking that perspective, one profoundly "masks
the existing, complex, and different class contradictions that cannot be reduced to the singular binary opposition of the interests of the 'blacks' and
those of the 'mulattoes'" (Labelle 1978, 14).

Insofar, then, as these ideologies of color had their origin during the
colonial period, I will start by summarizing the class and racial system of
Saint-Domingue on the eve of the slave uprising in 1791. At the top of the
class and racial/color hierarchy were the white French planters who owned

the majority of the 793 large sugar plantations and most of the 455,000 slaves in the colony. For the most part the large planters settled in the colony permanently to form the dominant class of Creoles, but a wealthy minority returned to France and left their properties to be managed by overseers or procurators. In France, these absentee planters became the allies of the maritime or merchant bourgeoisie in control of the colonial trading system. Together, the resident Creole planters, the absentee owners, the representatives of the merchant bourgeoisie, and the colonial administrators formed the ruling class of *grands blancs* or "big whites."

Immediately below the class of *grands blancs* was a middle class comprising owners of smaller cotton, cacao, indigo, and coffee plantations, and fewer slaves than the large sugar planters. The significant characteristic of this class is that it included white Creoles and members of the *affranchis* or "free people of color" population of mixed European and African origins, most of whom were classified as mulattoes. Even though mulattoes served as the reference group for the "people of color," as they were called, many freed blacks also belonged to that class.[1] The free people of color came into their own as a class during the so-called coffee revolution of the 1750s and 1760s, when, as a by-product of the racial discrimination they suffered at the hands of whites, they retreated into the interior and hilly areas of the colony, where they were able to acquire or take possession of unclaimed lands to cultivate coffee and other crops. The *affranchis* owned not only property but slaves as well. By 1791, in fact, they owned up to one-third of the productive properties, and one-fourth of the slaves of the colony, making them a significant bloc of property owners. In addition to the property and slave owners, the middle class included professionals such as physicians, lawyers, retail merchants, colonial military officers and administrators, shopkeepers, and self-employed craftsmen and artisans. Again, within this group were to be found both whites and *affranchis* (mulattoes and blacks). There was also a white and *affranchis* working class of skilled and unskilled workers, sailors, store clerks, and apprentices, coachmen, and dockworkers, among others. Taken as a whole, the whites who belonged to the middle and working classes formed the *petits blancs* ("small whites") of the colony, so-called because they distinguished themselves from the *grands blancs*, whom they opposed politically, and the class of *affranchis*, whom they despised because of the immediate competition they faced from that group for access to employment, property, and other positions in the colonial administration and the colonial militia.

Below the dominant, middle, and working classes that made up the free population of Saint-Domingue and numbered some 40,000 whites and 28,000 free people of color were the approximately 455,000 slaves, the vast majority of whom were black. The slaves worked primarily as laborers on the plantations, but also as domestic servants and in the myriad jobs that whites and *affranchis* considered below their dignity to perform. As I showed in chapter 1, it is they who turned Saint-Domingue into the wealthiest colony of the Caribbean by outproducing all the French and English colonies combined and earning Saint-Domingue the designation as the "pearl of the Antilles" and the envy of all other Caribbean colonies in the eighteenth century (see Dupuy 1989, 21–22).

The class system of Saint-Domingue, then, did not exclude free mulattoes and blacks from the ranks of property and slave owners. By contrast, the racial system that slavery engendered worked to exclude free mulattoes and blacks socially, politically, and even economically from certain occupations such as medicine, law, or any public function, thereby depriving the *affranchis* of the powers and privileges commensurate with their class standing. As in all other New World slave societies of the eighteenth century, the institutionalization of a racial hierarchy made it possible for whites of any class to assert their social supremacy over blacks or mulattoes of any class to constitute what came to be known as *l'aristocratie de la peau* (aristocracy of the skin) or simply white supremacy (Cournand 1968). Whites, however, did not have a monopoly on the exercise of skin privilege in the colony. It may not always have been easy to distinguish between mulattoes and blacks or between mulattoes and whites, but mulattoes practiced their own racism against blacks by excluding blacks from their social networks and intermarrying among themselves or with whites if possible. The *affranchis* also defended slavery, but free blacks were not allowed to buy mulatto slaves. Mulattoes who were slaves not only were treated differently from black slaves but also considered themselves superior to blacks (Labelle 1978, 51; Garrigus 2006, 51–81).

Achille Mbembe expressed that racial construction well:

> Blackness does not exist as such. It is constantly produced. To produce Blackness is to produce a social link of subjection and a *body of extraction*, that is, a body entirely exposed to the will of the master, a body from which great effort is made to extract maximum profit. As exploitable object, the Black Man is also the name of a wound, the symbol of a person at the mercy of the whip and suffering in a field of struggle that opposes socioracially segmented groups

and factions. Such was the case for most of the insular plantocracies of the Caribbean, those segmented universes in which the law of race depended as much on conflict between White planters and Black slaves as between Blacks and "free people of color" (often manumitted mulattoes), some of whom owned slaves themselves. (Mbembe 2017, 18, emphasis in original)

The system of racial stratification, therefore, straddled and contradicted the class system in Saint-Domingue, in such a way that in the vertical divisions of class emerged an impermeable horizontal racial division among whites, mulattoes, and blacks. The ideologies of race and racism, therefore, became parts of the system of social class and class closure to enable whites to monopolize the positions of power and privilege in the colony.[2] But while the racial order unified whites against mulattoes and blacks, it did not change the class divisions between whites. In fact, by creating a sense of solidarity among whites, the racial system reinforced the dominance of the *grands blancs* over the *petits blancs* and prevented the latter from challenging the former by forming an alliance with the mulattoes, with whom they shared much in common. At the same time, mulattoes who opposed the racism of the whites and fought to achieve equality with them also despised the blacks and defended the slave system. They, therefore, could not turn to the blacks to unite with them to oppose slavery and the racial system until they realized that freeing the slaves was in fact the only way they could win their own freedom from racial exclusion and oppression. As Aimé Césaire put it so poignantly, "the black stain of the mulatto, indelible as it must be, must mark his place. Forever" (Césaire 1960, 14).

Thus, even though the "race question" cannot be reduced to the "class question," it cannot be understood independently of the system of class relations in a specific society at specific points in time. Individuals with the same skin color may be classified differently depending on their structural location or class position in different societies. This explains why the construction of a system of racial/color hierarchy and the elaboration of ideologies of racial/color differences to justify the unequal positions of members of such racial/color groups differ from society to society, or even within the same society to reflect the shifts in the structural location of and power relations among different groups. Put differently, class divisions cut through racially designated social groups, and race/color relations never exist independently of class relations. Practices of racial distinctions and racism, therefore, always articulate with other class practices and their economic, political, and ideological manifestations in a specific society in the context of that society's position in the hierarchical international division of labor of the capitalist world econo-my (Dupuy 2014, 7–32). In other words, visible physical differences by themselves do not explain racism. Barbara Fields expressed this point suc-cinctly when she wrote that "race is not an element of human biology . . . nor is it an idea that can be plausibly imagined to live an eternal life of its own. Race is not an idea but an ideology. It came into existence at a distinctive historical moment for rationally understandable historical reasons and is sub-ject to change for similar reasons" (Fields 1990, 101; also cited in Dupuy 2014, 11).

In the case of Saint-Domingue, then, the class relations and divisions between the property owners, the middle classes, and the slaves came to express themselves as relations between *grands* and *petits blancs*, *affranchis*, and slaves, with their corresponding identification of freedom and privilege with whiteness, unfreedom and servitude with blackness, and something in between for the *affranchis*. Or, again as Césaire put it, the colonial slave system was "more than a hierarchy; it was an ontology: on top, the white—the *human being* in the full sense of the term—and below, the black, with no juridical personality, a furniture; a thing, that is, *nothingness*; but between this all and this nothingness, there was a forbidding in-between: the mulatto, free man of color" (Césaire 1960, 11). The balance of class forces between masters and slaves, and between whites, *affranchis*, and slaves determined the significance of the race question, and not the other way around. It is precisely because the class divisions expressed themselves in terms of racial/color divisions and generated such intense hatred and conflicts between them that they would engulf Saint-Domingue into one of the most violent and bloodiest civil wars the Caribbean has ever known, and to which I now turn.

As I mentioned in the previous chapter, the outbreak of the French Revo-lution in 1789 had a direct impact on events in Saint-Domingue, as did the latter in France, and brought into the open the contradictions and conflicts between different factions of the white Creoles, the *affranchis*, the leaders of the revolution, and the slaves. Inspired by the success of the American Revo-lution, factions of the resident Creole planter and middle classes saw an opportunity to push for greater autonomy and even outright independence from France. Other factions, however, especially those allied with the French merchant bourgeoisie and their representatives in the colony, continued to support the colonial administration and ties with France. The *affranchis*, especially the mulattoes who owned property and slaves, also saw the oppor-tunity to advance their cause by pressing their claims for full equality with the whites. They demanded that the Declaration of the Rights of Man and the Citizen decreed by the French National Assembly be extended to them as well. What is particularly noteworthy here is that despite these differences, the whites and mulattoes remained united on the question of slavery. Indeed, mulattoes such as Julien Raimond, a wealthy land and slave owner and advocate for mulatto rights, especially those of his class, argues that to deny the *affranchis* equal rights with the whites would destroy whatever opportunity existed for an alliance between the "free classes" on the question of slavery and prevent a full-scale uprising by the slaves (Raimond 1793).

For their part, if the whites were divided on the question of autonomy or independence from France, they remained united not only on the question of slavery but on the necessity to preserve the system of white supremacy that guaranteed their power and privileges in the colony. From the standpoint of the whites, granting equality to the people of color would threaten the entire social order and inevitably bring about the emancipation of the slaves. "Mulattoes today, slaves tomorrow!" exclaimed a spokesman for white interests (Le Noir de Rouvray 1959). The position of the whites in the colony also resonated in France, where the leaders of the revolutionary government were fully aware that to tackle the question of slavery and full equality for the *affranchis* would jeopardize the prosperity of the French merchants, the slave traders, the planters, and hence the French economy itself. Thus, they avoided the issue altogether.

Carolyn Fick argues that not one of the leaders of revolutionary France, or members of the Jacobin clubs, including Robespierre, Camille Desmoulins, and even Marat, wanted to touch the burning question of slavery and the slave trade until the slave uprising in Saint-Domingue in August 1791 gave them no choice (Fick 1997, 52–53). Césaire, on the other hand, claimed that of all the French revolutionaries in the Legislative Assembly or the National Convention who either sided with the colonialists against the mulattoes and the slaves, or supported the demands of the mulattoes and even the abolition of slavery while preserving the colonies, Marat was the only one who articulated a consistent anti-colonial and anti-slavery position, including the right of the colonies to revolt against the metropole and declare their independence, and the right of the mulattoes and blacks to revolt and even massacre the white colonialists to gain their liberty and their rights.

Indeed, as Marat expressed it in *L'Ami du Peuple*:

The foundation of all free governments is that no people is by right subjected to another, that it must not have any other laws than those it gives to itself, that it is sovereign domestically, and sovereign and independent from all human powers. [The white colonists who foolishly] agreed to send representatives to the French National Assembly have the right to emancipate themselves from the yoke of the metropole, to choose another sovereignty, or to erect themselves as a Republic since the supremacy that the metropole pretends to have over them is usurped, is based on maxims of despotism and is exercised only by virtue of the right of the more powerful. Given that our colonies are within their rights to emancipate themselves from the metropole, it does not follow that I am in favor of the white colonists: yes, without a doubt, they are inexcusable in my eyes for wanting to erect themselves as tyrannical masters of the blacks. If natural rights precede those of societies, and if the rights of men are imprescriptible, the rights that the white colonists have toward the French nation, the mulattoes and the blacks have them toward the white colonists. To shake the cruel and shameful yoke under which they lament, they have the right to use all possible means, even death, even if they must be reduced to massacre the last of their oppressors. (cited in Césaire 1960, 156–57)

The initial response of the French government to the slave uprising was to take a half measure on behalf of the *affranchis* in Saint-Domingue by declaring that those born of free parents would be given equal rights with whites. Even though this decree affected a small minority of the *affranchis*, white Saint-Domingue went mad, unleashing a wave of terror against mulattoes, and even threatening to secede from France unless it rescinded the decree. Mulattoes mobilized to defend their interests and raised their own militia in the face of steadfast opposition and hostility from the whites. As the revolution in Saint-Domingue spread further, the French government tried again to appease the revolutionaries by granting full equality to all *affranchis*, but the whites in the colony would have none of it and renewed their offer to England to take possession of Saint-Domingue. England, which along with Spain was at war with France, sent an expeditionary force to Saint-Domingue in 1793 and occupied the West Province and most of the southern part of the colony.

Granting equality to the *affranchis*, however, was all well and good for them, but it did nothing for the slaves, who were now determining events in the colony. Realizing this, and in order to stop the defection of rebelling slaves over to the Spanish army in neighboring San Domingo, which was attacking the French forces in Saint-Domingue, the French government declared that all slaves who joined the French forces in Saint-Domingue would be freed, and in August 1793 the French commissioners in Saint-Domingue abolished slavery altogether. By taking these actions, the commissioners dealt a fatal blow to the white colonists, who now pinned their hope on the British and Spanish forces to restore slavery and white supremacy in the French colony. Even though the abolition of slavery threatened the property interests of mulatto slave owners, the defeat of the white supremacists allowed the mulattoes to assert their power, especially in the southern part of the colony. Mulatto ascendancy, however, was short lived, as the entry of Toussaint Louverture on the political stage in 1794 shifted the balance of power decisively in favor of the black revolutionaries.

David Geggus pointed out that henceforth the "rest of the history of the colony, indeed that of independent Haiti, may be viewed as a struggle between the emergent power of the black masses and the predominantly brown-skin middle class" (Geggus 2002, 14). More in line with Labelle's point earlier, I would argue instead that the struggle was between an emergent black middle class during and after the war of independence and the old mulatto propertied class, on the one hand, and between both of them and the black masses, on the other hand. Between 1794 and 1800 a complex struggle unfolded between various factions in the colony that would determine who would finally control it. Spanish and English forces had invaded Saint-Domingue, and the goal of the English was to transfer the colony to England and restore slavery. The Creole planters and whites in general supported the English invasion, even though they would have preferred to become autonomous if not independent from France. The *affranchis*, especially the mulatto property owners who had gained full equality, aspired to become the dominant class and considered themselves the most "natural" and "capable" leaders because they were indigenous to the colony. This self-ascribed description would in fact become the rallying cry of the mulattoes in post-independent Haiti in their struggle for power with the black faction of the dominant class formed during and after the revolution. The French colonial officials sought to repulse the foreign armies to regain full control over the colony. To that end they enlisted the support of black and mulatto leaders in the colonial army and promoted them to officer ranks.

For their part, Toussaint Louverture and other black officers also aimed to control the colony. Having first defected to the Spanish side, Louverture agreed to join the French army, but only on the condition that the French government would ratify the decree of the civil commissioners that abolished slavery in 1793. When the French government finally did so in February

1794, Louverture moved over to the French army with the rank of general and brought with him a seasoned army of former black slaves. Louverture moved quickly to get rid of his opponents, real and suspected. Among others, they included Villate, the mulatto leader who in 1796 attempted a coup d'état aimed at blocking Louverture's ascendency by arresting General Etienne Laveaux, the only remaining officer in control of French forces in the North; the French civil commissioner Léger Félicité Sonthonax, who had devised the plans for the economic reorganization of the colony and whom Louverture accused of wanting to declare the independence of Saint-Domingue; the French general Thomas Hédouville, whom he accused of wanting to instigate discord between whites and blacks in 1798; General André Rigaud, the most powerful mulatto leader who launched a civil war against Louverture between 1799 and 1801 but lost and was arrested and deported to France; and, finally, Philipe Roume in 1800, the last remaining French official who opposed Louverture's objective to take over Spanish San Domingo and consolidate his power. These measures allowed Louverture and other high-ranking black officers who controlled a formidable army of ex-slaves to become the uncontested dominant forces in Saint-Domingue. The army also extended its control over the civil administrations of the various departments, and in effect imposed a military dictatorship in the colony with Louverture as its governor (Ardouin 1958, 3:59, 4:95; Cabon 1929, 4:195, 3:148–58, 4:24–27; Dorsinville 1961, 196; James 1963, 146–66, 239–40, 255–57; Jean-Baptiste 1957, 194–98; Lacroix 1820, 2:45; Pluchon 1979, 219–20, 270; Schoelcher 1889, 98–119).

Even though they did not declare the independence of the colony, Louverture and his revolutionary army were fully aware that by deporting all the representatives of the French government and taking over all the military and administrative posts, they had in fact broken the old relations with France and imposed their autonomy. In a letter he wrote to Napoléon Bonaparte in February 1801, Louverture informed him that he intended to maintain full relations with France, but that he was now fully in charge. As Victor Schoelcher, a biographer of Louverture, put it, this letter "bluntly announced to the First Consul that Toussaint had made a veritable coup d'état" (Schoelcher 1889, 287).

As governor of the colony, Louverture had a twofold objective. He wanted to make the former slaves of Saint-Domingue French citizens, keep Saint-Domingue as a French colony but one that was self-governed, and preserve the plantation system and the trade and economic ties with France.

Louverture believed that Saint-Domingue could not go it alone and that consequently the connections with France had to be maintained. He also realized that for his project to succeed, it was necessary to allow the former French planters to retain control of their properties and for the former slaves who had abandoned them to return to work on them. Many planters had fled the colony, however, and those who did not return had their properties seized by the new government and turned over to military officers who were now in charge of running them. The difference between this new regime and the old slave regime was that now the freed workers would be paid for their labor.

For Louverture the prosperity and the freedom of the colony were tied to the development of agricultural production. He therefore opposed the break-up of the plantations and the creation of a system of subsistence farming as the former slaves aspired to. To maintain order and the plantation system, Louverture imposed harsh discipline on the laborers and confined them to their plantations. At the same time, he adopted a conciliatory attitude toward the French planters who remained in the colony. Louverture knew that he could not trust the French planters because they were without principles and were only interested in their properties. But he needed them because they had the knowledge, experience, market connections, and capital the colony needed to prosper. Louverture also appointed many whites to administrative positions in his government. In general, the whites came to realize that Louverture could be trusted to protect their interests and many returned to the colony to regain control of their properties.

As James points out, however, Louverture was no naive politician. As the unchallenged master of the colony in 1801, he was well aware that the whites had no choice but to accept his regime; that the planters hated the laborers; and that they and the maritime bourgeoisie in France were anxious to return to the old regime. Nonetheless, James maintains, Louverture "set his face sternly against racial discrimination. He guarded his powers and the rights of the labourers by an army overwhelmingly black. But within that wall he encouraged all to come back, mulattoes and whites. The policy was both wise and workable, and if his relations with France had been regularized he would have done all he hoped to do" (James 1963, 261).

The laborers that Louverture had compelled to return to the plantations did not see things that way, however. They opposed Louverture's policies toward the French planters because they believed that he favored them more than the laborers and because they feared that the French wanted to reinstate the old regime. So deep was the resentment of the laborers against Louverture that they rebelled against him in the North Province under the leadership of Moïse, who was also commandant of the province. The aim of these laborers was not only to massacre the whites in the province, but to overthrow Louverture's government and replace him with Moïse. Understanding what was at stake, Louverture attacked and suppressed the rebellion, arrested Moïse, and had him executed. Louverture's opposition to Moïse was not only that he sided with the laborers in the insurrection; Moïse also favored the breakup of the plantations and their parceling into small farms that would be redistributed to junior officers and the rank and file. Thus, it was not so much that Moïse was anti-white as he was opposed to their continued exploitation of the laborers and Louverture's support of them. At issue, therefore, was the fundamental class question that was being decided, namely, who would dominate the colony and in whose interest it would be reorganized. Thus, when Louverture had Moïse executed the laborers thought of him as favoring the whites over them, and they never forgave him for this crime (see also Fick 1990, 207–10).

In addition to the conflict between Louverture and Moïse—as the representatives of the contradictory interests and the fundamental conflict between the newly emerging ruling class and the former slaves, respectively—over the question of maintaining the plantation system or transforming it into a self-subsistent farming economy, another conflict was emerging between Louverture and Jean-Jacques Dessalines, one of the top-ranking generals in Toussaint's army. At question here were the different attitudes of these two revolutionary leaders toward the whites in Saint-Domingue, which came to a head when Bonaparte sent an expedition to Saint-Domingue in 1802 to recapture the colony from Louverture and restore the slave regime. Instead of declaring independence immediately once he learned of the expedition, James points out, Louverture should have called the population to arms to resist Bonaparte's army and given the French planters the choice to either leave the colony or accept the new order and defend it. Instead, Louverture tried to maintain order and reassure the whites that they and their properties were safe. Instead, James goes on to say, Louverture should have spoken to the masses to explain to them what was happening and what needed to be done. For it was what the masses thought that mattered then, and not what the imperialists thought. As James put it, "if to make matters clear to [the masses] Toussaint had to condone a massacre of the whites, so much the worse for the whites. He had done everything possible for them, and if the race question occupied the place that it did in [Saint-Domingue], it was not the fault of the blacks" (James 1963, 286–87).

Louverture, however, explained nothing to the masses or even to his general officers; and by leaving them in the dark he drove them further away. James concluded that this was a regrettable and fatal error, a tragedy that could have been easily avoided, especially because he believed that "between Toussaint and his people there was no fundamental difference of outlook or of aim" (James 1963, 286–87). For James, then, Louverture's error was that he misunderstood the significance of the race question at this juncture in the conflict. As his frequently quoted but misunderstood passage put it: "The race question is subsidiary to the class question in politics, and to think of imperialism in terms of race is disastrous. But to neglect the racial factor as merely incidental is an error only less grave than to make it fundamental" (James 1963, 283). James believed that Louverture understood that the race question is a political and social question, but his mistake was to deal with it in those terms and to ignore the fears and feelings of the former slaves while at the same time appearing to be taking the side of the whites. By so doing, James concluded, "Louverture committed the unpardonable crime in the eyes of a community where the whites stood for so much evil. That they should get back their property was bad enough. That they should be privileged was intolerable" (James 1963, 284).

As with James, Césaire also argues that "if Toussaint's ideas were good, his method was much less so. The most delicate problem for a revolutionary is that of his relation with the masses, it requires flexibility, inventiveness, a sense and awareness of the human. And that is where Toussaint failed. Fighting a war day and night, he had a military outlook, which was mechanistic and schematic. He succumbed to that. He stopped inventing, content to apply to all new situations the military model he had mastered. He believed he could solve everything by militarizing everything" (Césaire 1960, 228).

James's and Césaire's arguments would have been more convincing, however, if in fact Louverture shared the same interests as the former slave masses while attempting to appease the French planters because of the importance of maintaining their properties and investments in the colony. But such was not the case. Louverture and the other high-ranking officers of the revolutionary army in charge of the colony in 1800 also took control of the properties of those planters who had left the colony, and by either leasing or buying them, they became a property-owning class in their own right. Louverture himself came to own several plantations, as did Dessalines, Moïse, and other high-ranking military officers. Military officers and administrators of the new political order not only appropriated properties from former French planters; they also despoiled the public treasury (Pluchon 1979, 287–92; Sannon 1933, 3:103).

By using their political, military, and state power to acquire wealth and property, the leadership of the revolutionary army and the new administrators of the colony transformed themselves into a new black propertied class alongside the old class of white and *affranchis* property owners. As such, this new landowning class sought to preserve the plantation system and transform the former slaves as laborers on the plantations. Given this to be the case, then, Louverture's error was not that he took the masses for granted, as James suggests, but rather that he believed he could convince the French colonial planters, and even Bonaparte, to accept the new social order he had created because he preserved Saint-Domingue's colonial status and defended the properties of the whites who remained. In other words, except for the question of emancipation and the formal equality of all blacks and whites, Louverture, as leader of an emerging black property-owning bourgeoisie, came to share the same interests as the white and mulatto property owners. And he hoped that Bonaparte would understand that this was a wise policy and would accept the new order to save the colony. In effect, Louverture was 145 years ahead of his time. In 1946 France incorporated its other colonies in the Caribbean (Martinique, Guadeloupe, Guyane) as overseas departments with full citizenship rights.

But in 1801 Bonaparte did not and could not see things that way, convinced of his invincibility and blinded as he was by his racism. In a letter he wrote to General Leclerc on July 1, 1802, he made it clear that Leclerc was to arrest and deport all the black generals to France because "without that we would have accomplished nothing, and a large and beautiful colony will always be a volcano, and would instill confidence neither in the capitalists, the colonists, nor commerce" (Bonaparte 1861, 7:503; see also James 1963, 217–75). Reflecting later on his defeat by the slaves of Saint-Domingue while languishing at Saint Helena, however, he wrote in his autobiography that

> the expedition of Saint-Domingue was one of the greatest acts of folly that I have committed. If I had succeeded, it would only have served to enrich the Noailles and the Rochefoucaulds. From the administrative point of view it is the greatest mistake that I have ever made. I ought to have treated the black chieftains as with the authorities of a province; I ought to have appointed

negroes [*sic*] as officers in their regiments, and made Toussaint-Louverture viceroy. Instead of sending troops I ought to have left everything to the black men. In this way the negroes would have acquired confidence in my policy. The colony would have announced the freedom of the slaves. (Bonaparte 1931, 104)

No doubt Louverture would have wished that Bonaparte had thought of this policy in 1800 as well. Unlike Louverture, however, Dessalines had a radically different attitude toward the French. He had no illusions about the French and did not have the slightest desire to accommodate or reassure them. He simply wanted them out of the colony. He did not care what the whites thought. And he had no hesitation as to what to do once the French military expedition arrived. He called on everyone, mulattoes and blacks, men and women, to rise together to oppose the French and drive them out of Saint-Domingue. Moreover, and equally as important, Dessalines came to believe that Saint-Domingue would have peace only after Louverture and everything French in the colony were gotten rid of. He had his plan for national independence ready long before the French expedition, and he was simply waiting for the right moment to act. After Louverture agreed to capitulate to the French in 1802, Dessalines and other generals plotted with General Leclerc, the French commander in charge of the expedition, to arrest and deport Louverture to France (Fauvelet de Bourrienne 1895, 92; James 1963, 333–34). With Louverture out of the way, Dessalines was now in a position to reorganize the revolutionary army, unite with the mulattoes, and prepare to drive the French out of Saint-Domingue for good. This realization of the common objectives of the leaders of the black and mulatto factions of the dominant class also gave rise to a new nationalist sentiment and identity among them.

The unity of the black and mulatto leaders now opposed to the French and determined to carry out the war of independence to its conclusion, however, had one other obstacle to overcome before they could do so. This was to convince the independent bands of guerrilla fighters to unite with the indigenous army rather than fight against it. Many such guerrilla bands operated independently in different parts of the country and opposed both the interests and objectives of the leaders of the revolutionary army since the rise of Louverture at the same time that they wanted to get rid of the French. These independent guerrilla bands, in other words, represented the interests and aspirations of the former slave masses.

Given that to be the case, if the unified revolutionary army under Dessalines and Alexandre Pétion (who succeeded Rigaud as the leader of the mulatto forces) were to succeed in defeating and driving the French from Saint-Domingue, it first had to defeat the guerrilla forces. Though some guerrilla groups agreed to join the revolutionary army, others steadfastly refused. They were subsequently attacked and defeated by the unified army, which then turned its guns on the French. By the end of 1803, the revolutionary army had defeated the French forces, declared the independence of Saint-Domingue, and renamed it Haiti on January 1, 1804 (Dupuy 1989, 72–74).[3]

At the heart of the difference between Louverture and Dessalines, however, were not only the ties with France, but which social class would become dominant in Saint-Domingue, or, after independence, in the new Republic of Haiti. Whereas Louverture opposed severing ties with France and Dessalines wanted independence, the two did not differ in their desire to maintain the system of plantation production and the transformation of the former slaves into a free wage-labor force. As with Louverture, Dessalines opposed the interests of the former slaves to become landowning farmers. Louverture, however, favored a nonracial solution to this problem by maintaining ties with France and forming an alliance with the former French planters and the old class of *affranchis* property owners. Dessalines, on the other hand, was concerned primarily with the interests of the newly emerging black propertied class, and therefore opposed the alliance with the French planters who would have remained dominant in the reorganized colony if Louverture's plan had succeeded. Dessalines's goal was to make the new black property owners dominant. Moreover, he knew that while he could get rid of the French by fighting for independence, the mulattoes were there to stay. Thus, he understood that a struggle between them and the new class of black property owners would become inevitable after independence. The mulatto leaders understood this as well. Therein lies the origin of the "color question" and its intimate connection to the "class question" that would unleash the internecine conflicts between the two factions of the dominant class that characterized Haiti's post-independence history and which I will discuss further in the next chapter.

My main point, then, is this: neither Louverture nor Dessalines defended the fundamental interests of the former slaves beyond the fact that they opposed the restoration of slavery. Both Louverture and Dessalines represented the aspirations of a newly emerging black propertied class that was created by taking over the lands confiscated from the French planters; both wanted to maintain power through military dictatorships; and both wanted to preserve the plantation system established by the French and convert the former slaves into a wage-labor force on the plantations. Louverture tried to create a black landed elite that would form an alliance with the former master class and the class of mulatto property owners. It was Louverture's hope that by promoting a black landed bourgeoisie equal in power to the whites and mulattoes, slavery and the system of racial stratification characteristic of the old regime could be dismantled without breaking the ties with the French economy deemed essential for Saint-Domingue's development. Although he did not take the final step toward independence, Louverture's program offered the possibility of a nonracial solution to the colonial question based on an alliance among those old French planters who would have accepted the new social order and lived with the old mulatto bourgeoisie and the newly formed black bourgeoisie as their equals. In other words, Louverture wanted to abolish the system of slavery and white supremacy, maintain the status of Saint-Domingue as a self-governed colony, and extend full citizenship to the former slaves and mulattoes alike. This was indeed a radical project that was ahead of its time, as I mentioned earlier. But in 1802 slavery and the system of white supremacy were essential to France, its merchant bourgeoisie, and its colonial planters, and Bonaparte could not contemplate such a proposition when he was at the height of his power.

When one combines this reality with the racism and opposition of the mulattoes on the one hand, and the aspirations of the black nationalist factions for complete independence on the other hand, it is not hard to conclude that Louverture's vision was doomed from the start. The elimination of Louverture, then, was the logical conclusion, and once this happened Dessaline's racially based nationalist alternative became realizable. Dessalines, as the representative of the nationalist faction he led, reduced the contradictions of the colonial regime to the divisions between whites and blacks rather than between property owners and laborers, as Louverture did. But even though he opposed ties with the French planters, Dessalines did not seek to break ties with foreign capital per se. He sought to have commercial relations with Britain and the United States. But unlike Louverture, he was unwilling to grant foreigners the concessions Louverture consented to. Dessalines's objective was to make the black elite the uncontested leaders of Haiti.

Notwithstanding the different approaches of these two leaders toward the French planters and France, they and the other leaders of the revolutionary government represented the emergence of a new indigenous bourgeoisie that sought to preserve the plantation system and the continued production of the export crops, principally sugar and coffee, that had made Saint-Domingue the wealthiest colony in the Caribbean before the revolution. The problem they confronted, however, was that the former slaves fought against their transformation into free wage-laborers to be exploited by a new class of indigenous property owners, whether mulatto or black.

With the whites out of the way, the acrimonious prejudices between mulattoes and blacks would resurface as a principal division that would underline much of the struggle for power between the two factions of the new dominant class in post-independent Haiti. As this occurred, the "color" question replaced the "race" question as the ideological battleground between the black and mulatto elites. In that context, the racist ideology developed during the colonial period to defend white supremacy became redefined and transformed into ideologies of "color" that undergirded the struggles between the two factions of the dominant class and the broader cultural struggles to define the meaning of nationhood and peoplehood in the new Haiti.

In short, then, the Haitian Revolution confronted and resolved two fundamental questions in the Caribbean: the questions of slavery and white supremacy. After the Haitian Revolution, it became impossible to justify the regime of slavery for very much longer, even though it would take another eighty-eight years to abolish it entirely in this hemisphere. And even in those Caribbean territories that remained under colonial rule until the twentieth century, the system of white supremacy vociferously defended during the period of slavery crumbled to give way to light- or brown- and dark-skinned elites long before the achievement of formal independence.

The Haitian Revolution, however, did not resolve the question of class exploitation that the slaves had fought against. On the contrary, it gave rise to a new, but divided, indigenous bourgeoisie that would exploit the subordinate classes and accumulate the wealth they produced as all capitalists do, while claiming to rule in the interest of "the nation." Having proclaimed the independence of that new nation on January 1, 1804, the task of the new bourgeoisie was to gain the recognition and legitimation of that status by the French and the other imperial powers who could not yet fathom the idea of dealing with a sovereign black nation as an equal among nations when they had hitherto considered black peoples as fit only to serve as chattels to white masters. The next chapter analyzes how the new Haitian bourgeoisie tackled and resolved that burning question.

NOTES

1. There is always a risk when talking about mulattoes to treat them as a homogeneous group. Mulattoes, or the "free people of color," differed in terms of skin color (from lighter to darker skin complexions) as in their social status. Though many among them were property and slave owners, others engaged in other occupations ranging from artisans to plantation overseers, to professional soldiers in the colonial militia, to semi-skilled and unskilled workers. A small number of mulattoes were slaves. In other words, they shared neither similar class positions, similar relations with the whites, nor similar interests or views on the burning questions of the day. Though most wanted equality with whites, not all of them supported equality for blacks, the abolition of slavery, or independence from France. Thus, when I speak of "mulatto" interests here, I am referring primarily to the interests of the property and slave owners and their leaders, even though divisions existed among them as well.

2. The concept of social closure is derived from Max Weber and refers to "the process by which social collectives seek to maximize rewards by restricting access to resources and opportunities to a limited circle of eligible citizens. This entails the singling out of certain social or physical attributes [such as race or gender] as the justificatory basis of exclusion" (Parkin 1979, 44).

3. See also Carolyn Fick's *The Making of Haiti: The Saint-Domingue Revolution from Below* (1990, 204–36) for an authoritative analysis of the conflicts between the slave masses and the revolutionary leadership, and the role they played in the struggle for independence and the making of the new nation of Haiti.

Chapter Four

Property, Debt, and Development

Rethinking the Indemnity Question

Every student of Haitian history knows that in July 1825 Haitian president Jean-Pierre Boyer accepted the ordinance of King Charles X of France, which stipulated the following conditions for the recognition of Haiti's independence:

> 1) The ports of the French part of Saint-Domingue will remain open to all nations. The duties collected at these ports, whether on the ships or on goods, whether incoming or outgoing, will be the same for those under the flags of all nations except for those under the flag of France and for which they will be reduced by half. 2) The inhabitants of the French part of Saint-Domingue will pay to France, in five equal installments the sum of 150 million francs intended to compensate the former colonial proprietors who demand to be indemnified. And 3) We concede, by the present Ordinance and under those conditions, to the actual inhabitants of the French part of Saint-Domingue, the full and complete independence of their government. (AP-1-20 *Ordonnance du Roi*, 17 avril 1825)

The 150 million francs was calculated to represent 10 percent of the properties of the colonists, including slaves, estimated to be worth some 1.5 billion francs on the eve of the Saint-Domingue Revolution. And from that sum, each of the 12,000 claimants approved by the commission that was created to distribute the indemnity among them (or their descendants) was to receive 10 percent of the total value of their loss, or approximately 1.2 million francs to avoid exceeding the total of 150 million (Ministère des

Finances 1834, VII–IX). It is also well known that in a second treaty with France in 1838 Boyer succeeded in reducing the total amount to be paid to France to 60 million francs with annual installments spread over thirty years; lowering the interest rate on the 30 million francs Haiti borrowed from a French bank to make the initial payment on the original 150 million francs indemnity from 6 to 3 percent; and eliminating the half duties Haiti had to pay on its exports to France, but which it had already stopped paying before the treaty. Haiti paid off the indemnity in full in 1883, that is, in fifty-eight years (forty-five if one bases it on the 1838 treaty) instead of thirty (MAE 47CP v. 8, *Ordonnance du Roi*, 30 mai 1838; Blancpain 2001, 63–74; Las Cases, AE-B-III-458, 4 mars 1838).

Historians generally agree on the following sequence that led to the final acceptance of the ordinance, much of it based on the report the baron de Mackau sent to the comte de Chabrol, the French minister of marine and the colonies, at the conclusion of his meetings with Boyer, as well as on the *Mémoires* of Joseph Baltazar Inginac (1843), Boyer's secretary-general. De Mackau arrived in Port-au-Prince on July 4, 1825, with a flotilla of fourteen French warships stationed off the bay of Port-au-Prince. He met with Boyer's emissaries: Inginac, Senator Rouanez, and Colonel Frémont. They raised objections to the first clause of the ordinance, which they interpreted as maintaining France's sovereignty over Haiti and giving it the right to inter-vene in its internal affairs as it pleased. They argued that as written that clause contradicted the third clause, which recognized Haiti's independence, and they replied to de Mackau's allusion to the use of force if the indemnity was not accepted that Haiti would defend itself against such aggression. The emissaries then briefed Boyer, who agreed with their reasons for rejecting the ordinance, but he agreed to meet with de Mackau alone. The first day of their meeting ended inconclusively. Boyer believed the 150 million francs indem-nity was far above the 80 million that had been stipulated during negotiations in 1824 and beyond Haiti's means, and that the tariff reductions France demanded were excessive and needed to be reduced (Etienne 1982, 112).

He eventually accepted those terms because, as he said, he "wanted to be done with it,"[1] but he maintained that he could not accept the first clause because it was an affront to Haiti's honor and the rights it had won and would defend. He then proposed to write to Charles X to ask him to clarify that it did not mean what he believed it did, after which he would accept the ordi-nance and get it ratified by the Senate. When they met the next day, de Mackau handed Boyer a note he had prepared in which he made clear that based on the directives he had received personally from the king before he left for Haiti, he could certify that the first clause did not in any way mean that France intended to maintain some sort of suzerainty over Haiti or the right to interfere in its internal affairs; that the notion of keeping all ports open to the flags of all nations was part of the agreement the independent powers of Europe had reached at the Congress of Verona in 1822; that the king of France was not trying to take away with one hand (i.e., the stipulations of the first clause) what he was granting with the other (i.e., the third clause, which recognized Haiti's full and complete independence); and that he was certain the amount of the indemnity and the tariffs could be renegotiated. But first and foremost, the ordinance had to be accepted and ratified as written.

De Mackau then made the following proposition: his orders were strict and he could not negotiate the terms of the ordinance.[2] But if Boyer accepted the ordinance and had it ratified, he, de Mackau, would stay as a hostage in Haiti and would send an emissary to France to get the certification Boyer wanted. Otherwise he would have to carry out his orders to their full extent, meaning the blockade of Haiti's ports until Haiti accepted the ordinance. This meant, of course, that France and Haiti would be at war. Boyer replied verbally and in writing that this would not be necessary; that he was satisfied with the explanation he was given; and that he would accept the ordinance. He then proceeded with its ratification by the Senate (Ardouin 1958, 9: 76–78; Boyer AP-1-20, 8 juillet 1825; Brière 2008, 112–14; Coradin 1988, 191–96; de Mackau AP-156-1-20, 7 juillet 1825; Etienne 1982, 112–15; Inginac 1843, 70–73; A. N. Léger 1930, 130–36; Madiou 1988, 6:448–63).

As would be expected, different interpretations of Boyer's decision to accept the ordinance abound. For example, Thomas Madiou concluded that de Mackau's "clarifications" to Boyer were nothing more than "an ultimatum sugarcoated with delicate and polite terms: it was either accept the ordinance or war." Boyer capitulated, according to him (Madiou 1988, 6:460). For Beaubrun Ardouin, Boyer had no choice but to accept the ordinance given the international context in which Haiti found itself. Great Britain and the United States, which were two of Haiti's most important trading nations since it became independent in 1804, had both refused to recognize Haiti's independence even though they had done so for the rebellious Spanish colonies in South America. Rejecting the ordinance could have led to war, even if there had only been talk of a blockade. He therefore sided with Inginac, who had advised him to accept it for the same reasons (Ardouin 1958, 9:88–89;

Inginac 1843, 71–72).[3] Jean Coradin advances a similar view. Boyer, he argues, was negotiating under pressure of a possible confrontation with France and knew that he could not count on the English or the United States to support him. The question was whether to risk a war for which he was not prepared or accept the ordinance: "everything seemed to suggest that it was to resolve that dilemma that he accepted the ordinance" (Coradin 1988, 197). Abel-Nicolas Léger was far more critical, arguing in effect that Boyer sold out: "Haitian diplomacy had capitulated on all points in 1825. Public opinion let Boyer and France know that the Ordinance of 17 April did not accord with its expectations. That moment marked the beginning of the tenacious opposition to Boyer that would culminate eighteen years later in the Praslin uprising" against him (A. N. Léger 1930, 141).[4] Victor Schoelcher advanced a similar view, arguing that Boyer "was afraid of the French flotilla, and that is why [Haitian] patriots condemned his pusillanimity and never forgave him for the way he concluded that negotiation" (Schoelcher 1843, 167). Likewise, Jean Price-Mars concluded that de Mackau had not been sent to Haiti to negotiate the terms of the ordinance but to impose them on the Haitian government. There was in this "non-negotiable approach all the appearance of an abuse of power. And also in the acquiescence of the Haitian government all the appearance of a capitulation, a capitulation to force" (Price-Mars 2009, 1:163).

Largely based on the same belief that Boyer was forced to pay the indemnity, former Haitian president Jean-Bertrand Aristide demanded that France repay Haiti the equivalent sum of $21,685,135,571.48 for the 90 million francs in a speech he gave on April 7, 2003, to commemorate the bicentenary of Toussaint Louverture's death. The reimbursement combined what Aristide termed *restitution* for the indemnity and *reparation* for the enslavement of Africans in Saint-Domingue (Aristide 2003). The French government predictably rejected Aristide's demands outright (Radio Métropole 2003). The French government then appointed a commission led by the well-known writer Régis Debray to issue a report to respond to Aristide's demands. The report disingenuously claimed that Aristide's demands had no legal standing because the right of nations to self-determination did not exist in 1838 (when France actually recognized Haiti's independence), and neither did the concept of slavery as a crime against humanity, which was not recognized as such until after World War II. Moreover, the report went on, France had offered substantial bilateral and international foreign aid to Haiti during the past century, but only to have it mismanaged (Debray et al. 2004). The

French government, however, had a more direct way of dealing with Aristide. A year after his demand, France joined the United States and Canada in supporting the organized opposition to Aristide and the rebel soldiers of the former Haitian army to topple and exile him, first to the Central African Republic and later to South Africa in 2004, where he remained until he returned to Haiti in 2011 (Caroit 2004; Dupuy 2014, 112–14).

FROM TOUSSAINT LOUVERTURE TO JEAN-PIERRE BOYER: THE MAKING OF A LANDED BOURGEOISIE

In contrast to the arguments summarized above that interpreted Boyer's acceptance of the indemnity as a capitulation or as having no choice but to do so, I will offer a different view that focuses instead on the *class interests* Boyer, and Pétion before him, were defending when they proposed to offer to pay an indemnity to compensate the former colonial property owners in return for France's recognition of Haiti's independence. As I pointed out previously, the "class question" since the time Louverture came to power in 1800 was inextricably linked to the "property question." The "property question," in turn, was linked to the seizure of the properties of the former colonialists and their redistribution by Louverture and the post-independence governments of Jean-Jacques Dessalines, Henri Christophe, Alexandre Pétion, and Jean-Pierre Boyer to create a new landowning bourgeoisie alongside the old property-owning *affranchis* class. And resolving the "property question," I will show in this chapter, was the principal reason Pétion first offered, and Boyer agreed, to pay an indemnity to France.

To be sure, the international context in which Haiti was operating was fundamental in their considerations. Haiti was heavily dependent on international trade and access to the markets of the advanced countries for its products. And given that neither the United States, England, nor any other major power was willing to recognize Haiti's independence before France did so gave the latter considerable leverage in its negotiations with Haiti. So frustrated was Boyer over France's refusal to recognize Haiti's independence that he asked in a letter he wrote on May 16, 1821, to Esmangart, a former colonist who had been charged with reopening negotiations with Haiti, "The efforts France made on its part to ensure Washington's triumph, did they not bring fame to the regime of Louis XVI? Impressed by these examples, Haitians are asking themselves often why that latter power hesitates to repudiate such vain rights to reap more honorable benefits. Could the difference in skin color be the reason for this hesitation?" (cited in Madiou 1988, 6:198–99).

Commenting on that letter, Madiou argues that skin color was not the issue. Rather, he suggests, France regretted relinquishing its once wealthiest colony in the New World and was attempting to "establish a protectorate in the interest of its preponderance in the Antilles and the Gulf of Mexico which centrally overlook the two Americas" (Madiou 1988, 6:198–99). No doubt, France could not come to terms with the loss of its most productive and wealthiest colony in the Americas. But the "race question" in fact could not be so easily separated from France's economic and political interests. As I will point out below, just as Bonaparte sent Leclerc to retake possession of Saint-Domingue in 1801 to restore slavery and the racial order of the colonial regime, so did King Louis XVIII attempt to reassert France's sovereignty over Haiti after it declared its independence in 1804. Except for reinstituting a full-scale slave system, his government sought to regain control of its former colony, return the colonial properties to their former owners, and reestablish the old racial order. These objectives were clearly laid out in the instructions that Pierre-Victor Malouet, a former colonist who was now minister of marine and the colonies, gave to the emissaries he sent to Haiti in 1814 to negotiate the terms under which they would surrender control of Haiti back to France with the governments of Alexandre Pétion and Henri Christophe.

As did Christophe, Pétion and Boyer consistently opposed all attempts by France to reimpose its sovereignty over Haiti before and after the 1825 ordinance even if that meant war. In 1824, after the emissaries he had sent to France failed to reach agreement on a treaty to recognize Haiti's independence in return for an indemnity and reciprocal commercial advantages, Boyer published the report of his emissaries and summarized the history of all the negotiations since 1814:

> In 1814, France sought to impose its complete sovereignty; in 1816, it was a question of a constitutional sovereignty; in 1823 the issue was limited to demanding the indemnity we had offered. Why return to the idea of subjecting us to an *external sovereignty* in 1824? What is this *external sovereignty*? From our point of view, it includes two types of rights: one is that of a protectorate; and the other concerns foreign relations, whether political or economic, both of which would then be asserted. But for whom is this *sovereignty* being thought of? However we think about this *sovereignty*, it seems to be injurious

or contrary to our security, and that is why we rejected it. (cited in Schoelcher 1843, 164–65)

Schoelcher pointed out that at this point the "French government understood finally that it either had to abandon all relations with the old colony or establish them on mutually recognized and agreed upon grounds. It is on that basis that Charles X [who succeeded Louis XVIII] issued the ordinance of 17 April 1825" (Schoelcher 1843, 164–65; addition mine). If that is the case, then, Boyer accepted the ordinance not because he feared war with France but because it was in his interest to do so. This was the only way, he believed, that both the property question that remained at the heart of the conflicts between the former colonial planter class and the Haitian bourgeoisie and the question of independence could be solved simultaneously. Moreover, by declaring the indemnity a national debt in 1826, Boyer saddled the nation with the bill, which meant that the people as a whole would pay the heavier price for servicing the interests of the bourgeoisie (AE-B-III-380, 25 Février 1826; Ardouin 1958, 10:6).

The formation of a new indigenous landed bourgeoisie began with the rise of Toussaint Louverture and his revolutionary army when they gained control of the colony in 1800.[5] That new sector of the dominant class would combine with that of the "free people of color," predominantly mulattoes but also blacks, who together owned approximately one-third of the productive properties—mostly coffee plantations—and one-quarter of the slaves before the revolution and the abolition of slavery in 1794 (Debien 1950, 214–15; Moreau de Saint-Méry 1797/1958, 2:1110, 1138, 1154–55; 3:1400). The revolutionary government had committed to maintaining the plantation system and for that to happen it needed to solve two problems simultaneously. The first was that many colonial plantation owners had fled the colony when the revolution broke out, an exodus that continued after Louverture took power in 1800. He encouraged them to return and resume control of their properties. Those who did not or could not because they had fled to a colony of a foreign power at war with France had their properties confiscated by the revolutionary government. Together these properties amounted to two-thirds of all the colonial properties under the old regime (Cabon 1929, 4:109; Gambart 1802; see also ch. 3).

The revolutionary government then put the confiscated properties under the control of military officers. Many also bought or leased those properties, among them Louverture and Jean-Jacques Dessalines (who would take over the leadership of the revolutionary army after the arrest and deportation of Louverture in 1802). Those officers who had not bought or leased properties but were put in charge of them eventually became their de facto owners. Moreover, if absentee planters returned to reclaim their properties, they were obligated to reimburse the tenants all their expenses to maintain, operate, or improve the properties during the owners' absence. Many of them could not afford to do so and consequently the tenants kept possession of them (Cabon 1929, 4:193).

The second problem the Louverture government faced was that of labor. Since slavery had been abolished and the former slaves refused to remain on the old plantations and sought instead to gain access to and cultivate their own land, the government took measures to force them to remain. To prevent the breakup of the plantations and parceling them into small farms, the government prohibited the sale of properties smaller than fifty carreaux (one carreau equals approximately three acres). Those who sought to buy land had to prove that they did not previously belong to a plantation, to prove that they had the means to buy the land, and to declare what crops they would produce on their land and the number of workers they could employ (Ardouin 1958, 4:69; Idlinger 1802).

The revolutionary government did not stop at those measures. It also issued a draconian decree in 1800 that sought to compel the former slaves who could not prove that they were duly employed or practicing a "useful occupation" to return to their old plantations or face arrest. In return for their labor, the workers would receive one-fourth of the net value of the crops produced in addition to being allowed to cultivate their own provision grounds. In effect, then, Louverture militarized the plantations. As Adolphe Cabon put it, under the military officers put in charge of running the plantations that had been abandoned by their former colonial owners, the workers were

> subjected to a servitude that was not the slavery of the old regime, but which must have appeared to them as severe as their old status. The name of slave was abolished, but the military discipline established throughout the country transformed the plantations into a battalion under a chief. [And] the laborer was constantly constrained to produce more and more, without any aim other than the prosperity of the plantation. (Cabon 1929, 4:189)

The post-independence governments of Jean-Jacques Dessalines, Alexandre Pétion, and Henri Christophe failed to deal successfully with either the property or the labor questions. Boyer definitively resolved the first question with the acceptance of the 1825 ordinance, but not the second. On the property side, Toussaint's government and those of his successors were committed to preserving the fundamental bourgeois concept of private property ownership. Consequently, the problem they confronted was that the expropriation, appropriation, redistribution, and even sale of colonial properties by these successive governments did not resolve the question of ownership insofar as the original titles for those properties remained in the possession of their former colonial owners or their inheritors. That is what the indemnity was meant to solve.

The defeat of the French forces at the end of 1803 led the victorious revolutionary army under Dessalines's leadership to declare the colony's independence and rename it Haiti on January 1, 1804. The war of independence, which lasted from August 1802 to December 1803, had been devastating in human and material terms. Claude and Marcel Auguste estimated that a total of approximately 150,000 people had been killed on both sides, and between 100,000 to 130,000 Haitians and 50,000 to 55,000 French had been permanently disabled. The cities of Le Cap, Port-de-Paix, Gonaives, and Saint-Marc had been burned to the ground, and throughout the country plantations, sugar mills, irrigation networks, wharfs, and other businesses had been destroyed, amounting to an estimated value of 1,144,258,948 francs. In essence, this meant that Haiti started off with a ruined economy and infrastructure (Auguste and Auguste 1985, 313–19; Dupuy 1989, 74).

Once in control of the state, Dessalines moved swiftly to consolidate his power by imposing a military dictatorship throughout the country and expulsing or killing the French who remained. French forces still occupied parts of Spanish San Domingo and were contemplating a new invasion of Haiti. Dessalines invaded that colony to crush them but returned soon after to prepare for another anticipated French attack that never materialized. In February 1804 Dessalines ordered the arrest, trial, and execution of all those French who had been found guilty of participating or assisting in the murder of blacks during the last two years under the control of Generals Leclerc and Rochambeau (Ardouin 1958, 6:14–17; Laurent n.d., 94–99; A. N. Léger 1930, 12–14; Placide 1826, 425–26).

The government then proceeded to confiscate all the properties that belonged to the French colonialists and declared them national properties, making this the most extensive nationalization of properties in the New World at the time (Mathon 1985, 34). As under Louverture, the new government leased the nationalized properties to functionaries and military officers who, as before, eventually acquired them. At the same time, laborers who had taken over abandoned properties and had no titles to prove ownership of those lands were swiftly dispossessed. Those who did not own land were also prohibited from cutting and selling logwood from public lands; only military and government functionaries could own and operate the mills on the properties allocated to them.

As Louverture did before him, Dessalines also compelled landless or otherwise unemployed laborers to return to their former plantations under military control. He took other steps to promote the rise of a black landed bourgeoisie by dispossessing mulattoes of lands sold or transferred to them after October 1802, primarily in the south where they were dominant. And the 1805 constitution, which declared in Article 6 that "property is sacred, its violation will be vigorously pursed," barred all foreigners (meaning whites of any nationality) from owning real estate property in Haiti. Article 12 further declared that "no white person, whatever his/her nationality, will be allowed on Haitian soil bearing the title of master or property-owner, and will be forbidden henceforth to acquire any property." Articles 13 and 14, however, made exceptions for white women and their children who became naturalized, and for naturalized Germans and Poles (Janvier 1886, 32).

Dessalines's discriminative, corrupt,[6] and repressive regime antagonized not only mulattoes but various sectors of the population, including factions of the military and the population, especially laborers and the landless. Henri Christophe, who was general in chief of the army, contemplated Dessalines's overthrow and even worked secretly with his arch-rival Alexandre Pétion to do so. An uprising erupted against Dessalines in October 8, 1806, quickly spread to different parts of the country with the support of sectors of the military, and ended with his assassination that same month (Ardouin 1958, 6:14, 33, 46–50; Dupuy 1989, 77–80; Laurent n.d., 128; J. N. Léger 1907, 158; Placide 1826, 434; Saint-Rémy 1956, 10:40, 45–47).

No sooner was Dessalines gone than a conflict erupted between the factions of the dominant classes allied with Christophe on the one hand, and Pétion on the other, which led to the partition of the country into two states. Christophe, who gained control of the North Province and renamed it the State of Haiti, had himself proclaimed king. He rallied behind him those who had risen to positions of power under Louverture's and Dessalines's respective governments and were predominantly black. For his part, Pétion took control of the west and the south,[7] and had the support of the predominantly mulatto bourgeoisie whose origins dated back to the colonial period before the rise of Toussaint Louverture. Neither Christophe nor Pétion pursued a "politics of color" *sensu stricto*; each appointed mulattoes and blacks to top positions in their respective administrations. But blacks benefited most under Christophe as did mulattoes under Pétion.

Christophe also attempted to revitalize the plantation system by putting military officers in charge or leasing the plantations to wealthy individuals or military officers so long as they kept them running. He also made land grants to lower-ranking soldiers (sergeants and lower), but in much smaller proportions than those granted to officers according to rank. He also compelled landless and mainly rural laborers to work on them and confined them to those plantations. As was the case under Louverture, they were to receive one-fourth of the value of the products and were allocated provision grounds; and he resorted to forced or *corvée* labor as well. Christophe also established commercial relations with Great Britain in an attempt to weaken France's influence and tried in vain to gain England's recognition of Haiti's independence. He gave foreigners who brought their businesses to his kingdom guarantees to protect their properties (Clarkson 1952, 47, 108–9, 268–71; Cole 1967, 209–10; Franklin 1828/1970, 201; Leyburn 1941, 45; O. E. Moore 1972, 25; Moral 1961, 31; Nicholls 1979, 52–53).

By contrast, Pétion was confronted with a peasant rebellion in parts of the southwest in 1807 that lasted until he died in 1818 and was not fully crushed until 1819 by his successor, Jean-Pierre Boyer. Consequently, Pétion pursued a more liberal land and labor policy than Christophe did in the north, using his agrarian policy as a weapon in his conflicts with the latter. In addition to returning to the mulatto property owners the lands Dessalines had taken from them, he preserved the lands that had been placed under the national domain. As his predecessors had done, he leased or sold public lands to high-ranking military officers and public officials. But he also made land grants to lower-ranking officers and mid-level civil servants, as well as to rural laborers. Nonetheless, the wealthiest landowners appropriated the best and largest properties and also benefited from tax exemptions on coffee and sugar production. Pétion himself took over the Ferron de la Ferronnays sugar plantation in the Cul de Sac (one of the most productive regions in the colony) and after his death in 1818 passed it on to Boyer, who also owned several other properties in different parts of the country (Cheney 2017, 211; Moral 1961, 40).

Pétion also pursued a more liberal policy toward the laborers. As with the previous regimes, laborers were still paid one-fourth the value of the crops and they were also granted their own provision plots. But the plantations were not militarized and workers could leave them with special permits to go beyond their parish. Vagrants were more harshly punished. In short, it could be argued that because of the more "liberal" nature of Pétion's regime, the repression of workers had to be opaque and shrouded in a greater appearance of liberality (Leyburn 1941; Manigat 1962; Moral 1961; Nicholls 1979; Péan 2000; Pierre-Charles 1967).

Rising to power in 1818 as president of the Republic of Haiti after Pétion's death, and of a reunified country in 1820 after Christophe's, Boyer reverted to the draconian land and labor policies of Louverture, Dessalines, and Christophe embodied in his 1826 *Code Rural*. As did those of his predecessors, Boyer's code declared that workers had an obligation to labor on and were bound to the plantations and were permanently assigned to them. Workers could not form cooperatives but had to sign contracts with the landowners and receive one-fourth to one-half of the gross revenues, or in some cases be paid in wages. Boyer, nonetheless, was unable to reconstitute the large-scale plantations of old, largely because to do so would have required the expropriation of the medium and small farmers who had benefited from Pétion's more liberal redistributive policies. By the time of the "Praslin Revolution" of 1843 that led to Boyer's overthrow and exile in March of that year, a significant opposition to Boyer led by the more liberal wing of the Haitian bourgeoisie had coalesced around a series of grievances that demanded an end to the government's authoritarian tendencies and repressive measures, greater freedom of the press and public debate, educational reforms, legislative reforms, and a coherent program of economic development and agricultural reform (Bellegarde 1938, 110–12; *Code Rural de Boyer 1826* 1992; Coradin 1988, 295–98; Franklin 1828/1970; Leyburn 1941, 66–70; Moral 1961, 41–43).

A QUESTION OF PROPERTY

After Bonaparte's defeat in Saint-Domingue, he turned his gaze on conquering Europe. But that did not work out for him either. His defeat at Leipzig in 1814 by the quadruple alliance of Austria, England, Prussia, and Russia led to the Paris Treaty of May 1814 and the restoration of King Louis XVIII and the Bourbon dynasty in France. A subsequent treaty in November 1815 reduced the size of France to its 1792 configuration, imposed an indemnity of 700 million francs to be paid to the allied powers in five years, and prohibited it from engaging in armed hostilities against other nations. But it allowed France to keep possession of the Caribbean colonies it still had in 1789, including Saint-Domingue. Moreover, an additional secret article to the 1814 treaty from the king of England granted France permission to continue the slave trade for five years and use "whatever means it chose, including armed force, to re-appropriate Saint-Domingue and bring it and the population of that colony under its obeisance." The article went on to stipulate that Britain "reserves the right of its subjects to engage in commercial transactions in the ports of Saint-Domingue that would neither be attacked nor occupied by French authorities" (CC9A-216 MIOM-34, 24 juin 1814; Coradin 1988, 64; France *Traité*, 20 novembre 1815).

France's defeats notwithstanding, its dispossessed colonial planters were pressing Louis XVIII to recolonize Haiti so they could regain possession of their properties and reestablish the old slave order. That objective was supported by Pierre-Victor Malouet, the new minister of marine (Clarkson 1952, 57). But France also knew that having won its independence through a revolution, Haiti would not allow itself to be recolonized peacefully. Since Haiti won its independence, England and the United States became its main trading partners, and French ships could come to Haiti only under a foreign flag. But neither of these powers, nor any other Western power, was willing to recognize Haiti's independence until France did so. For the United States in particular, doing so would have meant legitimizing a slave revolution, thereby undermining its own slave regime and its concomitant ideology of white supremacy. But the United States went further than refusing to recognize Haiti's independence. It also actively pressured the other newly independent states of Latin America, including those revolutionaries like Simon Bolivar to whom Pétion had offered material and military support in his struggle for independence, not to recognize Haiti's independence and to exclude it from participating at the Panama Congress of 1826 (Coradin 1988, 141–44; Dupuy 2014, 57). The solidarity among the imperialist powers and the diplomatic isolation of Haiti, therefore, weighed heavily on the new republic and would be highly significant in Boyer's decision to accept the 1825 ordinance.

It is in the context outlined above that one can best understand France's strategy to reassert its dominance, both political and economic, over Haiti. Seeking to exploit the divisions between Christophe and Pétion, the French government dispatched three emissaries, Dauxion-Lavaisse, Franco de Medina, and Draverman to Haiti in July 1814. They were to deal, respectively, with Pétion, Christophe, and Borgella. As I noted in note 7, however, the latter had submitted to Pétion in 1812 and no longer controlled any territory, a fact that France obviously did not know (Wallez 1826, 12–13). This meant, then, that the emissaries would be dealing with Christophe and Pétion. Malouet gave the three emissaries specific instructions to try to persuade both leaders to submit peacefully, but they were also to inform them that if they were uncooperative France was ready to use force if necessary.

France's objectives were unambiguous. Seeking to exploit the color divisions and the rivalries between the two factions of the dominant class, the instructions outlined seven key strategies: (1) mulattoes whose complexions are proximate to those of whites would be fully assimilated and granted more privileges similar to those accorded to whites; (2) the rest of the mulatto caste would be granted political rights but with some exceptions that would keep them subordinate to whites; (3) all others whose complexions are less proximate to whites would have lesser rights; (4) all free blacks would have fewer advantages; (5) all blacks who were currently working on plantations, and those who freed themselves from those obligations, would be reassigned to their old plantations; (6) blacks who could not be freed but were considered too dangerous would be expelled from the colony; and (7) the number of those who would be freed would be limited.

Once these conditions had been met and agreed upon by the current rulers, the following conditions would be added: (1) property rights and all those that guarantee them must be reestablished and respected, such that all those former colonial owners who had titles, inherited them, or had notary certificates of ownership, would regain possession of their properties; (2) all peoples of color would have political rights and the property owners among them would be assimilated, as long as it was understood that such rights and those who would fulfill higher or lower positions in the civil administration and the military were not acquired rights but were granted at the discretion of the king. Those who are currently in charge of the colonial government would submit to the authority of the king, and they would assure those members of their castes who obey them of the good graces of the king, but without imposing any obligations or demands on his authority. Once these conditions were met and the current heads of the colonial government certified their submission in writing, they would be freed of all future responsibilities ("Instructions," in Wallez 1826, 186–89).

Christophe and Pétion responded differently to these revelations. Christophe disdained the French, favored closer ties with England, and was seeking its recognition of Haiti's independence, as I mentioned above. When Medina crossed into Christophe's domain from Santo Domingo, Christophe had him captured and brought to Cap Haïtien. Malouet's instructions were found on him. He was interrogated, jailed, and executed.[8] Christophe then published all the documents Medina was carrying, and sent them, including Medina's interrogation, to Pétion. He in turn sent them to Dauxion-Lavaisse, who acknowledged their authenticity. With the real intentions of France exposed, Pétion asked Dauxion-Lavaisse to leave Haiti (Wallez 1826, 13–17).

During his monthlong stay in Haiti, Dauxion-Lavaisse and Pétion exchanged many letters in which Pétion made it clear that Haiti would never accept any form of French suzerainty and demanded nothing less than France's recognition of Haiti's independence. But in his last letter to Dauxion-Lavaisse of November 27, 1814, Pétion offered what seemed to be an unsolicited quid pro quo: that in "recognizing the rights and independence of Haitians," Haiti would in turn "reconcile with what it owes to certain of the King's subjects[9] [and] work to establish the grounds for an agreed upon indemnity that we will agree to pay" ("Pétion to Dauxion-Lavaisse," in Wallez 1826, 166–70; also cited in Ardouin 1958, 8:23). As Inginac—who served under both Pétion and Boyer—noted in his *Mémoires*, Pétion made the offer of an indemnity "for the properties of the old colonists who were henceforth barred from the country, so that the free and independent Republic could deal with France as one nation to another, otherwise war between the two countries would be interminable" (Inginac 1843, 29).

In early October 1816, the French launched new initiatives to attempt to regain control of Haiti. In a series of exchanges between the French emissaries Esmangart and François Fontanges and Pétion, they tried to convince him to accept French sovereignty over Haiti—which they referred to as "this colony"—by arguing that a country can consider itself independent only if it is able to defend itself from external threats without having to rely or depend on the support of another power. Given that Haiti did not have the means to do so they considered its independence to be a mere "pipe dream and a pretention it could not sustain." Pétion replied that Haiti would never compromise its independence and accept French rule, even if this meant war and the destruction of its society and economy. He broke off negotiations with the French envoys (FCO Haiti and President: Pétion 1816, no. 14, 38–39). For his part, Christophe, who had been reassured by Thomas Clarkson that

France was not in a position to launch a military invasion and that any such consideration "would be considered to be mad . . . and as hopeless and disastrous as the Expedition of Leclerc," simply refused to meet with the French envoy (Blancpain 2001, 48–49; Clarkson 1952, 200).

Boyer became president of the republic after Pétion died in 1818, and of the entire country in 1820 after Christophe's suicide. He pursued Pétion's principle of rejecting any form of suzerainty over Haiti but was also willing to offer to pay an indemnity to France in return for its recognition of Haiti's independence. And, as Pétion had also done, Boyer twice broke off negotiations with France before 1825. The first was in 1821 with the French envoy Dupetit-Thouars, who continued to insist on subjecting Haiti to French sovereignty. Among the main reasons Boyer wanted to bring Spanish Santo Domingo under Haitian rule in 1821–1822 were to counter French threats to use Santo Domingo's ports as bases for its ships, troops, and supplies; to abolish slavery and liberate that colony's blacks and mulattoes; and to have more land to distribute to compensate revolutionary war officials (Fisher 2004, 170).

The second time was in 1824. In an address to the nation on October 18, Boyer announced that he had ended negotiations with France. Reiterating the offer Pétion had made to pay a "reasonable" indemnity to France, he also made it clear that Haiti would accept nothing less than "the full and complete recognition of its independence free of any and all foreign domination, suzerainty, or protectorate by any foreign power." Haitians, he went on to say, would "never deviate from their resolve, and if ever they had to repulse an unjust aggression once again . . . they would [vigorously] defend the independence [they had won] and enjoyed for the past twenty years" (*Pièces officielles* 1824).

Even though the former colonial property owners were clamoring for France to retake possession of Haiti, Boyer knew that France was no longer seriously contemplating, or, more to the point, capable of launching another Napoleonesque military expedition, given the balance of forces between France and the other European powers and the enormous loss in both manpower and military equipment such an undertaking would entail (Eugène 2003, 145–46; Price-Mars 2009, 1:154). Thus, as Price-Mars noted, all France could do was "to engage in diplomatic maneuvers camouflaged as coercive threats to regain a foothold" in its former colony (Price-Mars, 2009, 1:154).[10] As Madiou pointed out, once France had learned that the country had been reunited under the leadership of Boyer in 1820, the question of how to deal with Haiti resurfaced. The chambers of commerce of the maritime ports of France recommended to the duc de Richelieu that France recognize Haiti's independence so that they could establish normal trade relations. Esmangart also advised Louis XVIII to do the same but in return for an indemnity for the colonial property owners, which Pétion had already proposed. In February 1821 Louis XVIII convened a private council to give him its advice on the "question of Saint-Domingue." The council's unanimous recommendation was that

> it was time to reject all military expedition aiming to re-conquer the old French colony because this would require the extermination of its entire population that was resolved to defend its liberty and its soil. [Now] that the slave trade had been abolished, France would not be able to repopulate it, and it would be impossible to keep secret such an expedition that would require incalculable expenses and a prior consent from the parliamentary assemblies; that it would also be useless to think of a blockade of the ports because that would interfere with trade and require the deployment of almost all of France's naval forces without any hope of success; and finally that Boyer and his fellow citizens would throw themselves into the arms of the English if they felt threatened. (cited in Madiou 1988, 6:193–94)

In a letter Thomas Clarkson also wrote to Boyer on May 25, 1821, he told him that

> with respect to France, it becomes you to be upon your guard. When I was at Paris last year, I understood that the French Government had given up all idea of trying to conquer Hayti by force of arms, but that they had not given up the idea of trying to obtain it by *intrigue*. [Y]et I am not sure that these continue to be their sentiments *at the present moment*. Opinions often change with circumstances. Your Revolution in Hayti has changed the face of things here; and, no doubt this revolution will frequently force itself upon the consideration of the French Government, with a view of inquiring whether it may not afford them new pretenses or opportunities for completing their wishes in that quarter. It becomes you, therefore, to be on your guard. (Clarkson 1952, 224–25, emphasis in original)

In his reply to Clarkson on July 30, 1821, Boyer acknowledged that

> it is certainly possible that France may insist on failing to recognize her own interests and refuse to profit by the lessons of experience, but I can assure you that any attempt she may take to enslave us would fail when directed against the strength of this government, which is built upon the solidarity and affection

of all Haitians. A long series of misfortunes has taught us that only we can guarantee our rights, and that we must be always on guard against the perfidious machinations of our enemies and the pitfalls they place along our route. (Clarkson 1952, 229)

Nothing had changed between 1821 and 1825, when Boyer accepted the ordinance. As for France's consideration of a massive military expedition similar to that of 1802, it had also become clear that, given the balance of forces internationally at the time, it was no longer possible for France to reconquer its old colony by military means (Eugène 2003, 145–46). What did change, however, was that Boyer himself altered the terms of the negotiations with France. In April 1824 he sent two emissaries to France (Larose and Rouanez) with a letter to Esmangart that "left no doubt about the clauses of a treaty they were to conclude, and the indispensable formality of the recognition, by a royal ordinance, of our absolute independence from all foreign domination, of any sort of suzerainty, in a word, of the independence that we have enjoyed for the past twenty years" (*Pièces officielles* 1824, 7).

Boyer's "Instructions" stipulated the following acts to be included in the ordinance:

1) A royal ordinance that recognizes Haiti's independence from France; 2) Once the ordinance is obtained, Haiti will offer an indemnity to France to be paid in five installments, either in Haitian or foreign currency, or in equivalent Haitian goods; 3) French commercial ships will be admitted in all commercial ports of the Republic with the same privileges granted to other favored nations; 4) Crops produced in Haiti (sugar, coffee, cotton, indigo, cacao) and other commercial goods will not pay higher fees than those that French goods would pay in Haiti; 5) That Haiti will remain neutral in case of war between France and other powers; and 6) That Haiti would welcome a French *chargé d'affaires* or a general consul, and France will do the same for Haiti. (*Pièces officielles* 1824, 51–56; also cited in Coradin 1988, 164–65)

In 1825, France issued just such an ordinance, but with different stipulations concerning the amount of the indemnity, which as I mentioned above had been set at 80 million francs in 1824, and the tariff concessions Haiti would grant to France and those Haiti would pay to export goods to France. Given that to be the case, and that de Mackau had signaled to Boyer that these terms could be renegotiated once the ordinance was accepted and ratified by Haiti, it would have been difficult if not impossible for Boyer to reject the ordinance he himself had requested. It is noteworthy that the baron de Las Cases, whom France sent to Haiti in 1837 along with Captain Charles Baudin and six naval warships to threaten to blockade Haiti's ports if it did not honor its payments on the indemnity, admitted in his *"Lettre tout à fait pour l'histoire"* that de Mackau's threat of a blockade in 1825 notwithstanding, Boyer accepted the ordinance only after he received the clarifications he had sought from the French emissary. Inginac also confirmed that this was the case. And de Mackau himself acknowledged in his report to the minister of marine and the colonies that in his meeting with Boyer's emissaries (Inginac, Rouanez, and Frémont) the threat of a blockade did not have "any effect on them as did the assurance I gave them [about the ordinance] and this is so true that I could have succeeded better if I had never talked of the squadron" (of fourteen warships), but he did so because those were his orders (de Mackau AP-156-1-20, 1825; Inginac 1843, 71–72; MAE-CP v. 7, 17 février 1838).

Boyer understood that the recognition of Haiti's independence stipulated in the third clause of the 1825 ordinance was conditional on Haiti paying off the indemnity in five years. He knew that this was impossible since he was compelled subsequently to borrow 30 million francs from a French bank at 80 percent to make the first payment in November 1825.[11] That transaction came to be known as the "double debt" Haiti incurred: the 150 million owed to France plus the 30 million from the French bank (Blancpain 2001, 66; Brière 2008, 162–63). Thus, as Price-Mars remarked, Boyer understood the burden he had assumed and set out immediately to renegotiate the amount of the indemnity and the other clauses of the 1825 ordinance dealing with trade, taxes, and duties to be paid to and received from France (Price-Mars 2009, 1:167). Many attempts at such negotiations took place between 1825 and 1838.

But one particular set of events was significant and had to do with a renewed French threat of war if Haiti refused to honor its obligations under the 1825 ordinance. In 1830, the July Revolution (also known as the "Second French Revolution") forced King Charles X to abdicate power; he was succeeded by his cousin Louis Philippe. In 1831 Boyer unilaterally eliminated the half-duties exemption on French imports. France responded by threatening war. At the same time, Saint-Macary, the Haitian envoy Boyer had sent to France, signed two financial and trade treaties with France. The first treaty kept the original amount of the indemnity and required Haiti to pay 4 million francs per year until it was paid off; it also demanded that Haiti reimburse France for the duties it had collected in violation of the 1825 ordinance, namely, the half duties on Haitian exports since 1827, and the half duties on French imports since 1831. The second treaty eliminated the half duties but allowed French citizens to engage in wholesale and retail commerce in Haiti as well as own and/or inherit real estate properties, a clear violation of the 1805 constitution. Boyer rejected both treaties and broke off diplomatic relations with France (Ardouin 1958, 10:30–37; Brière 2008, 222–23; Madiou 1988, 7:93–95).

Acting on instructions he received from France, Mollien, the French consul in Haiti, threatened military action against Haiti. Boyer responded by putting the army on alert. He also ordered the construction of a new city, Pétion-Ville, in the hills above Port-au-Prince and out of reach of French gunships, where government archives, military arsenals, and supplies could be secured, and, if necessary, the seat of government could be relocated (Brière 2008, 219–25; Madiou 1988, 7:97–104; MAE 47CP, v. 5, 19 juin 1831; Price-Mars 2009, 1:176)). The next major tension in Franco-Haitian relations came in November 1837 when France sent two commissioners, the baron de Las Cases and Captain Charles Baudin, and again threatened to blockade the ports of Haiti and Santo Domingo[12] if Haiti did not pay the indemnity according to its means. Boyer again responded that Haiti was open to negotiating with France but would not do so under the threat of war and would defend its independence to the death (Briére 2008, 240–43; Madiou 1988, 7:202–3).

As I mentioned earlier, by February 1838 Haiti and France signed two treaties. In the new treaties, France recognized Haiti as a free, sovereign, and independent state, and treated trade between the two countries on the same basis as those considered most favored nations. And the indemnity was reduced to 60 million francs to be paid in yearly installments over the next thirty years. But Haiti did not do so until 1883 (that is in forty-five rather than thirty years) when President Lysius Salomon exclaimed that "I paid France the last term of the double debt of 1825" (cited in Turnier 1985, 27). The treaties also lowered the interest rate on the 30 million francs Haiti borrowed from a French bank to make the initial payment on the original 150 million francs indemnity from 6 to 3 percent. As such, the indemnity Haiti was now obligated to pay to France was reduced from 150 million to 90 million francs: the 30 million borrowed for the first installment in 1825 plus the 60 million agreed to in the 1838 treaties (Blancpain 2001, 63–74; Madiou 1988, 7:214–15; MAE 47CP v. 8, *Ordonnance du Roi*, 30 May 1838; Montague 1940, 85–87).

Boyer's gambit paid off, at least on the diplomatic front. By May 1826 Great Britain recognized Haiti's independence and sent a consul, Charles Mackenzie, to Haiti. Other European countries followed suit and also sent consuls to Haiti, including the free Hanseatic cities of Bremen and Hamburg along with the Low Countries, Hanover, Prussia, Sweden, and Norway. In 1839, England invited Haiti to subscribe to the treaty it had concluded with France to suppress the slave trade, which Haiti did after France made the same request (Brière 2008, 154; A. N. Léger 1930, 201). Speaking about Haiti's international standing after 1825, A. N. Léger, who had been critical of Boyer's "capitulation" to France, admitted that "Europe was beginning to show particular interest to us. The end of our quarrel with the old metropole was slowly making the horizon clearer. With international peace, we would be better able to mark our place in global activities" (A. N. Léger 1930, 201–2).

Based on the foregoing analysis, then, it is clear that Boyer did not accept the 1825 ordinance because he feared war with France. This is so for two reasons. The first is that Boyer knew that France was not contemplating or preparing for a massive military expedition to reconquer Haiti. The second is that although a blockade was an act of war and could have caused serious disruptions to international trade with Haiti, to be effective it would have needed to be expanded to all Haitian ports, and indeed throughout the entire island of Hispaniola—that is, including the Spanish colony—which was under Boyer's control at the time. In fact, as I mentioned previously, one of the reasons Boyer decided to unify the eastern Spanish colony of Santo Domingo with Haiti was to prevent France from using it to threaten Haiti's sovereignty. At the same time, he informed the other European powers that he had no intention of using Haitian troops to help abolish slavery elsewhere in the region (Moya Pons 1998, 119–24; Price-Mars 2009, 1:172–73; Walker 2019, 15). Given that to be the case, to regain possession of Haiti, France would have had to deploy a much larger French fleet "without any guarantee of success" as the independent council appointed by Louis XVIII had concluded in 1821. There was no evidence that France was preparing to or could do so, and that is probably why de Mackau remarked in his report (cited above) that Boyer's emissaries did not seem concerned about his mention of a blockade.

If the fear of war was not the principal reason Boyer agreed to pay the indemnity, two others were. The first, as I have argued, was the desperate need for Boyer to gain official recognition of Haiti's independence by other

powers and become accepted as a legitimate nation. But those powers, especially the major Western powers and the United States, maintained their
solidarity with France and refused to do so first. The second reason also has
to do with legitimacy, namely, that of private property ownership. Beaubrun
Ardouin was one of the historians of the times who understood the reasons
Pétion and Boyer made their offers of a quid pro quo to France to recognize
Haiti's independence in return for an indemnity for the former colonial property owners.

Many have argued, Ardouin points out, that the colonial property owners,
or their heirs, had no right to receive an indemnity for the loss of their
properties, and neither should France in return for its recognition of Haiti's
independence because the horrible and criminal colonial regime forced Haitians to take up arms to win their freedom and their independence, and
therefore they had the right to exclude the colonialists and their ilk among
them. All that is true, he maintained, because the right to independence is
indisputable, as is that of excluding the former colonists to preserve Haiti's
liberties (Ardouin 1958, 8:23–24). But, he countered, enlightened "men"
must preserve what is sacred.

> And *property* is one such case because it is really the basis of all social order,
> old or new. A colony founded by a nation can resist oppression by its metro-
> politan power, take up arms against it, conquer its country to become a free,
> distinct, and independent and sovereign people, and exercise all rights over all
> goods in that country; but on the condition that it respects all that concerns the
> private rights of individuals.
>
> However, if, motivated by political considerations this new people deems
> it necessary to *exclude* certain private individuals from its midst, it has the
> right to do so; but it is obligated to *indemnify* them for the properties they
> owned legally and which had been taken from them by necessity. Because *all
> rights demand a corrective duty*; otherwise it is not *a right*, but *violence*, which
> can only be fought against and annihilated by a superior force. (Ardouin 1958,
> 8:23–24, emphasis in the original)

It would have been useful to enunciate these principles, Ardouin goes on
to say, to "prove the *injustice* of the critiques of Pétion for having proposed
the indemnity: those who advanced these criticisms failed to think through
that question." But what gave a country the right to found a colony in the first
place? Ardouin did not consider that question, but it lies at the heart of the
matter here. Had he done so, he would perhaps have realized that the colonists whose properties he believed should be indemnified because they were

taken from them by force had themselves not only expropriated the lands of the indigenous Taino population of Ayiti, but exterminated them. That genocide was first carried out by the Spanish, who were subsequently displaced by the French when they took possession of the western third of Hispaniola and renamed it Saint-Domingue. They then brought slaves from Africa to labor on their plantations, whose revolution in 1791 ended that criminal and brutal system (see chs. 2 and 3).

What "sacred" principle of property applied, then, other than that of "might makes right"? B. Vendryes, a former colonist, expressed that point succinctly:

> Saint-Domingue, this island of Haiti, had its part in the cruelty and injustice of which America was the theater and the victim.
>
> From the first days of its discovery, Christopher Columbus had been held accountable and sent to Spain.
>
> It was for this that a venerable bishop, Barthelemy de Las Cazas [*sic*], in his ill-considered pity, thought to buy African slaves. A vain and fatal measure! These poor, harmless, even hospitable inhabitants of Haiti disappeared no less to the last man, and 30 million [*sic*] of Africa's children perished in the fields of America.
>
> The buccaneers, these bandits that we could not hate, committed atrocious crimes against the Spaniards in Saint-Domingue, these victims we could not feel sorry for.
>
> If Saint-Domingue achieved a high degree of prosperity, it is due in part to the slave trade, until recently an object of the ambition of France and England, encouraged by the laws of the time, justly done away with and considered criminal by current laws.
>
> Their fortunes only lasted so long: the Constituent Assembly started it, the Convention hastened it,[13] and the empire completed the ruin of the old colonists of Saint-Domingue (Vendryes 1839, 1–2; also cited in Joachim 1971, 360–61; addition mine).

It is clear, then, that the "sacred principle" of private property to which Ardouin refers was neither inviolable by those who believe in it when it served their purpose, nor was it the foundation of all social order (in place and time). If only to cite the example of the precolonial period, the indigenous Taino Arawak society of Ayiti that I talked about in chapters 1 and 2 was hierarchical but it had no concept of, and was not based on, a system of private property ownership. Land was owned in common, and all the members of the society had access to its resources (Dupuy 1976). By contrast, private property ownership is the fundamental principle of capitalist society.

As Marx has shown in Volume I of *Capital*, without private property in land, labor could not be expropriated and prevented from having access to the means of production and self-reproduction; there could be no production of surplus value (profit) by the laborer and no accumulation of capital (wealth) by and for the capitalist. In short, there would be no capitalism (see ch. 1).

Returning to Ardouin and his attempt to justify Pétion's (and subsequently Boyer's) offer for the indemnity for the former colonial owners, he takes the latter's right to private property as a given and not as an expression in law of a set of relations of power, of social property relations, and of the production of commodities and wealth for a specific class of property owners through the exploitation of the propertyless. That is why he concluded his remarks on the indemnity by saying that, by offering it, Pétion (and hence Boyer) "acted in the *real interest* of the people" (Ardouin 1958, 8:23–24). Yet he himself had documented the opposite: that the policies of all the rulers from Toussaint Louverture to Jean-Pierre Boyer (and since) prioritized their own interests and those of the dominant classes who benefited the most from the confiscation and redistribution of the colonial properties, albeit to a lesser extent under Pétion, and who used such properties to (try to) compel the laborers to work on them.

Be that as it may, the key issue here is that Pétion and Boyer, both of whom (as did their predecessors) believed in the bourgeois right to private property ownership, sought to legitimize the redistribution of the properties expropriated from the old colonial property owners to create a new landed class in Haiti. And they saw no other way to do that than by offering to pay an indemnity to the former colonial owners, even if other members of that class did not understand it that way. I therefore agree with Jean-François Brière that accepting to pay the indemnity was not the price paid for the recognition of Haiti only, but that "it was in reality a massive transfer of property to the mulatto and black elite" (Brière 2008, 156; AE-B-III-380, 25 Février 1826). Jean Coradin came to a similar conclusion: "The ordinance of 17 April, by abdicating French sovereignty over its old colony, virtually ratified the ownership by Haitians of the properties of the former colonials" (Coradin 1988, 202). Paul Cheney also made the same point when he wrote that the "indemnity paid to the former plantations owners of Saint-Domingue can be seen, from a certain perspective, as a gentlemen's agreement between successive landholding elites" (Cheney 2017, 211). In a disingenuous, yet partly true, diplomatic note he sent to Boyer, King Louis Philippe, who himself had threatened military action against Haiti for not honoring its debt obligations, remarked that "if the indemnity was the price for the recognition of Haiti, the King's government, as much in consideration of the Haitian nation as for the respect for the rights of peoples, could have relinquished it; but it was accepted for the respect of private property" (cited in Ardouin 1958, 8:24n1).[14]

That is exactly how the expropriated colonial property owners saw it, namely, that by accepting the indemnity and refusing to conquer Haiti so they could regain their properties, their own government had betrayed them and they were the major losers in this deal. This was because, as I pointed out above, the total value of their properties in 1789 had been estimated at ten times more than the 150-million-franc indemnity that was based on the value of the revenues of their properties. Clément du Doubs, an advocate for the former colonists, expressed their grievances thusly: the ordinance of 1825, he argues, "effectively expropriated the legitimate property owners who had no recourse. Haitian law excludes them from owning property in Haiti. King Charles X acted as the agent of the former colonists, but sold their properties for less than one-tenth of their value; it negotiated to receive political and commercial advantages; the property-owners were forced to submit to the will of the government; they turned over their property titles in order to be paid [but] that payment would become illusory" (Doubs 1830, 3–4, 8–9).

Désiré Dalloz and Associates, consultants for the dispossessed colonial property owners, offered one of the clearest explanations of the meaning and implications of the indemnity. First, in recognizing Haiti's independence, it made it possible for it to henceforth gain the recognition of the other imperial powers, which had hitherto refused to do so before France, and to establish normal diplomatic and commercial relations with them (and other nations). Haiti's status therefore changed from a de facto to a legitimate and rightfully independent nation (Dalloz et al. 1829, 20). This was a primary objective of all Haiti's rulers since independence, from Dessalines to Boyer, all of whom categorically rejected any form of French suzerainty as nonnegotiable.

Second, the indemnity settled the question of property once and for all. It is true, Dalloz and colleagues argue, that the 1825 ordinance does not mention the transfer or the alienation of the private properties of the former colonial owners. Nonetheless, this is what the ordinance did, both in terms of the properties that were sold or given to private individuals by the Haitian state, and those that became part of the national domain, that is, public property. The indemnity that the Haitian government agreed to pay, then, was to ensure that the ordinance that also recognized its independence was simultaneously a "transfer of the property titles henceforth non-transferable and free from all French inheritance in Saint-Domingue." In other words, with the ordinance, the French government legalized "the dispossession of the former colonists which implied the voluntary renunciation of their properties" (Dalloz et al. 1829, 19–30; also cited in Coradin 1988, 202). But it did not only legalize the dispossession of the former colonists. As Joachim noted, insofar as recognizing Haiti's independence "entailed the sacrifice of the properties of the [colonists] without their consent, by taking this measure of expropriating them for the public good, the French government became the debtor of the expropriated" (Joachim 1971, 366) whether or not the Haitian government fulfilled its obligations toward France.

DEBT, POLITICS, AND DEVELOPMENT

The 90 million francs indemnity (60 million plus the 30 million borrowed in 1825 for the first payment on the original 150 million francs) that was finally paid off in 1883 represented about ten years of fiscal receipts for the Haitian government, heavily dependent at it was on customs duties for its revenues. Some, like Jacques Barros (1984), Leslie Péan (2000), Itazienne Eugène (2003), Paul Farmer (2003), Frédérique Beauvois (2009), Anthony Phillips (2009), and Eddy Toussaint (alias Tontongi) (2010) have argued that the indemnity and the burdens it inflicted on Haiti were a root cause of its inability to develop its economy in the nineteenth century and beyond.

Barros believes that the indemnity had serious consequences for all sectors of the Haitian economy (1984, 203). Farmer thinks that its "impact on nineteenth century Haiti was devastating" (2003, 7), whereas Péan says that it was the principal cause of Haiti's inability to develop its economy in the nineteenth century or since because it prevented the government from being able to lay the "foundation for an accumulation that could have led to some type of development" (2000, 245). For Phillips, the "independence debt drained the Haitian treasury of its capital. The Haitian economy—ravaged by war and long cut off from export markets—could not generate enough revenue to support the Debt" (2009, 7–8). For Beauvois, the indemnity "devastated the economy of the young republic. [It] became hostage to the debt and [it] was a clear strategy by the old metropolitan power to maintain its unofficial hegemony on the rebellious colony [and] place [Haiti] under France's economic grasp" (2009, 119). And for Eddy Toussaint (alias Tontongi), "the indemnity irreversibly affected Haiti's development by putting the country in a vicious circle of indebtedness, impoverishment, authoritarianism, and dependence on the imperialist powers, notably France and the United States" (2010, 2).

It is undeniable that the indemnity was harmful, insofar as it saddled a country with limited resources with paying a debt that was agreed to by its rulers (Pétion and Boyer) primarily for their benefit and those of the ruling class to which they belonged; and it was a decision in which the people had no say. The indemnity debt was unpopular among many sectors of the population and initially sparked protests in Port-au-Prince and an uprising in Cap Haïtien that was quickly suppressed. As Joachim points out, the indemnity was also unpopular among sectors of the dominant landed and commercial bourgeoisie, who were unhappy to see their rents and profits eroding for the benefit of French capitalists, and many of them used that excuse to blame the poverty of the people on the indemnity and turn them against the government (Joachim 1971, 362). And, as A. N. Léger mentioned earlier, it may have played a role in the uprising against Boyer, which in effect started at the end of January 1843. Boyer resigned on March 13 after the forces led by Rivière Hérard reached the city of Léogâne (about 29km/18 miles west of Port-au-Prince) on March 5 (Etienne 1982, 169).

Yet it is worth noting that in the *Acte de Déchéance* (Bill of Impeachment) issued by the leaders who led the uprising and forced Boyer to resign, no mention was made of the indemnity among the charges brought against him. Rather, the act accused him of cronyism and abuse of power; illegally removing senators from office; selecting candidates for the Senate who would do his bidding; using his authority to pardon and issue paper money; compelling the Senate to grant him powers he did not have under the constitution to form an army or to change the monetary system and suspend civil laws; unilaterally changing the tax laws; changing laws and refusing to observe those enacted by the Senate; denying citizens access to due process and judges and subjecting them to arbitrary judgments by civil or military commissions he controlled; removing judges arbitrarily and replacing them with those loyal to him; and arbitrarily firing civil employees and public functionaries (Hérard 1843; also in Madiou 1988, 7:474).

Boyer's fall, however, did not lead to an end in the grievances of other sectors of the population, especially the black factions of the bourgeoisie whom Christophe had favored. No doubt the mulatto faction benefited most under Boyer, and his fall rekindled the "color question," especially since Rivière Hérard, who succeeded Boyer, was a mulatto. Lysius Salomon, a large black landowner, mobilized farmers and their allies in the national guard and launched an insurrection against Hérard in 1843, but it failed. Soon after, the peasants in the backcountry of the southern city of Jérémie known as the *piquets*—they used wooden pikes as weapons—and led by Jean-Jacques Acaau rallied other laborers of the region behind them and toppled Hérard's government in 1844. That rebellion would not be complete-ly suppressed until 1848. Subsequently, three black generals, Philippe Guer-rier, Louis Pierrot, and Jean-Baptist Riché, ascended to the presidency con-secutively between 1844 and 1847. This strategy of electing black presidents came to be known as the *politique de doublure* (government by understud-ies), which essentially meant that to placate the popular demands for black presidents, the mulatto faction of the bourgeoisie helped elect them on the racist assumption that they could manipulate them. That strategy clearly failed, however. Guerrier died in office one year after he became president (1844–1845). Pierrot was overthrown after one year (1846–1846), and Riché also died within a year of taking office (1846–1847; Dupuy 1989, 97–98, 118; Trouillot 1990, 125–28).

Notwithstanding the internecine conflicts between the different factions of the bourgeoisie, its inability as a class to proletarianize the peasants and lay the basis for a more robust development of the Haitian economy weak-ened them vis-à-vis foreign capital and their governments. That is why I agree with Alain Turnier (1985, 27–42) that the "double" indemnity debt was not the primary cause of Haiti's inability to develop its economy. To recall the point David Harvey made in the first chapter, the processes and structures of uneven geographic development that characterize the capitalist world economy are constantly being renegotiated and are contingent on the particu-lar class configurations and social relations of production, the nature of the state and form of governance, the relative strengths of the ruling classes, and the alliances they form with other class factions or those of other states, the results of which facilitate or impede national development.

Those are exactly the conditions Haiti faced after it became independent and especially since 1843. On the one hand, the inability of the ruling class to proletarianize the majority of the producers compelled it to accommodate itself to the new configurations of the laboring classes that resulted from the struggles between them since the rise of Louverture, but especially during the early decades after independence and the different mechanisms of surplus extraction and capital accumulation this entailed. It also meant, on the other hand, that the ruling class had to renegotiate its relations with foreign powers and foreign capital from a relatively weak position resulting from the divisions and internecine conflicts among them. The combination of these factors lay at the root of the country's political and economic inertia of the nineteenth century.

As mentioned earlier, the respective governments of Dessalines, Pétion, Christophe, and Boyer tried to revitalize the colonial plantation system by transforming the former slave masses and their descendants into wage-laborers to work on them, whether they were paid wages or in kind, or a combination of both. But they all failed to do so on a scale large enough to restore the plantations and reach their previous levels of productivity. Boyer's draconian policies embodied in his 1826 *Code Rural* were the last attempt by the post-independence ruling class of Haiti to maintain the plantation system and the colonial model of production, capital accumulation, and economic development in the nineteenth century.

The former slaves and their descendants fought against their proletarianization and the consolidation of landed property by the dominant class. They succeeded in gaining access to land and their own means of production and reproduction by producing crops for their own consumption as well as for the local, national, and world markets. This explains why coffee supplanted sugar as Haiti's principal export crop in the nineteenth century. In 1790, Saint-Domingue produced a total of 163 million pounds of sugar and 77 million pounds of coffee. In 1818, Haiti produced 6 million pounds of sugar and 30 million pounds of coffee. In 1845, Haiti exported 42 million pounds of coffee, 68 million pounds of logwood, and 7.9 million feet of mahogany. And by 1859 Haiti ranked fourth among the world's coffee producers behind Brazil, Java, and Ceylon. In 1891, exports consisted of 79.3 million pounds of coffee, 1 million pounds of cotton, 3.35 million pounds of cacao, 90,000 pounds of raw sugar, 165.4 million pounds of logwood, and 35,000 feet of mahogany. Coffee exports during the nineteenth century accounted for 20 to 35 percent of the gross national product, and an average of 70 percent of the value of its exports. The producers of those crops, however, were not proletarians but farmers and peasants with differential access to land and hence different forms of exploitation or surplus extraction by the bourgeoisie (Girault 1981, 56, 58; Joachim 1979, 202; Moral 1961, 47–48; Turnier 1985, 47–48).

Sugar production, in effect, disappeared from some of the most fertile regions in the west and south of Haiti. In the Cul-de-Sac region, which had some of the largest and most productive sugar plantations during the colonial era, only a small number remained, operating on the basis of wage-laborers. The reason for the near disappearance of sugar plantations is simple. As I showed in chapter 1, sugar production required large plantations, a large quantity of labor, and an infrastructure, such as a water supply and equipment to harvest and transport the cane to the refineries to transform the cane juice into sugar, and to transport the sugar to the ports for export. Coffee, on the other hand, was perfectly suited to small family farms and required no significant investment in infrastructure or technology.

That failure did not alter Haiti's position in the capitalist world economy as a producer of agricultural crops and other raw materials for export, principally coffee, cacao, cotton, and lumber. As Marx pointed out, it is immaterial whether commodities are produced by wage-laborers, slaves, or peasants, as long as those commodities are produced for the world market and the surplus value embodied in them enters into the circuits of industrial capital and the circulation of commodity-capital. Thus,

> the process of production from which they originate is immaterial. They function as commodities in the market, and as commodities they enter into the circuit of industrial capital as well as into the circulation of the surplus-value incorporated in it. It is therefore the universal character of the origin of commodities, the existence of the market as world market, which distinguishes the process of industrial capital. What is true of the commodities of others is also true of the money of others. Just as commodity-capital faces money as commodities, so this money functions vis-à-vis commodity-capital as money. Money here performs the functions of world money. (Marx 1976, 1:110)

Be that as it may, the inability of the dominant classes to expropriate the immediate producers gave rise to different social relations of production between them and subordinate classes, which also implied different modes of surplus production, extraction, and capital accumulation by the bourgeoisie. The bourgeoisie comprised both urban and rural members. The former included the urban residents and owners of the larger private enterprises (industrial, financial, and commercial), the holders of state power and high government functionaries. That component of the bourgeoisie, especially those in the private sector, accumulated their wealth directly from the exploitation of the urban proletariat. The landed rural bourgeoisie consisted of those who owned the larger estates (ten or more, up to fifty to one hundred carreaux). They usually hired managers to run their properties, or they leased them to tenant farmers. Their wealth, therefore, derived from the rents of their properties. They also engaged in financial activities as moneylenders or speculators. They were essentially a rentier class that appropriated its wealth from the peasants' rents, buying their crops, and reselling them on the national and world markets, or from speculation.

Below the bourgeoisie was a middle class comprising the educated or credentialed cadres (lawyers, judges, medical doctors, engineers, the members of the intelligentsia, high- and low-ranking military officers, and public functionaries), both urban and rural. Such as it was, the proletariat in Haiti remained confined primarily to the urban centers and comprised both skilled and unskilled workers, public and private sector employees, domestic servants, and a large pool of unemployed workers or reserve army of labor. Together the urbanized classes represented between 10 and 15 percent of the total population (Adam 1982, 23–25; Bellegarde 1938, 159; Joachim 1979, 133–35; Luc 1976, 59–62).

The vast majority of the population, therefore, remained rural. But it was also divided into different classes and strata. Three categories of landed peasant farmers emerged: those who owned land (i.e., had legal titles); those who possessed but did not own land (i.e., had de facto but not de jure ownership); and those who leased land through the *métayage* or sharecropping system from large landowners. Those peasant farmers who owned/possessed land were also those who had larger, though still relatively smaller farms of approximately four to seven hectares (1 ha = 2.5 acres). Though there are no precise data on their percentage of the farming population, the "middle-class" landowners/possessors were a minority among the peasantry as a whole and were generally more secure financially and more independent because they also owned their tools, equipment, and draft animals. The second category of peasant farmers was those who could be considered the "small" peasants and made up the majority. They did not have land titles but possessed them and enjoyed full rights to their lands. They could not sell those lands but could bequeath or sell the "right of possession" to others. The lands possessed by these farmers were not always contiguous and were also parceled out to several inheritors, fragmenting them into even smaller plots.

The third category of peasants were either tenant farmers or sharecroppers (*métayers*) who leased land from the landed bourgeoisie, who subdivided their estates into smaller units, or from the state. The distinction between tenant farmer and sharecropper is important because the former tended to pay a fixed rent to the landowner in advance for a year or more. By contrast, sharecroppers paid their rent in money or in kind at the time of the harvest, and their rents tended to be higher than those of the tenant farmers. It could be said, then, that sharecroppers were more exploited by the landowners than were the tenant farmers, though either of them could be evicted for nonpayment of their rents.

Lastly, below the three categories of peasants described above were the landless or rural proletariat who sold their labor to those with land and were paid in kind or in money. It is important to note that many of the small peasants or tenant farmers unable to earn enough from their own land were compelled to produce cash crops (primarily coffee), hire themselves out to the middle peasants or the large landowners as day laborers, and must therefore be included among the rural proletariat (Barros 1984, 1:385–88; Bellande et al. 1980, 33–42; Dartigue 1938, 37; Dupuy 1989, 99–103; Girault 1981, 95–97; Joachim 1979, 126; Léopold-Hector 1977, 6–7; Luc 1976, 36; Lundahl 1979, 264; Millet 1978, 18–21; Moral 1961, 179–81).

A NOTE ON DEMOCRACY

As I mentioned above, the state became an important avenue of ascension to the dominant class for the factions that controlled it. The part of the surplus value produced by the laboring classes that it appropriated from the population from various property, import/export taxes, and rents was used to pay the salaries of government and public officials and to sustain the military and all other public expenditures (roads, ports, public education, etc.). By itself, the military, which was the principal means of accessing and maintaining power by the factions that controlled it, absorbed an estimated 20–27 percent of the national budget in the nineteenth century, reducing revenues that could have been used to promote social and economic development (Delince 1994, 44; Moïse 1988, 62). Michel-Rolph Trouillot expressed that point succinctly:

> From a structural point of view, the state functioned as an economic agent (extracting and redistributing the surplus) for the benefit of the local agents of dependence. These agents in turn exported most of the surplus, together with the local goods. As a result, capital accumulation by either the state or the strata that furnished its personnel (army officers, landowners, and professionals) was well-nigh impossible. (Trouillot 1990, 71)

One of the ways Haitian agriculture could have become more capital intensive would have been to transform the tenant farmers into capitalists alongside the landowners. Doing so could have been the basis for the creation of a domestic market for the production of agricultural equipment, machinery, and consumer goods, all of which, in turn, could have been the basis for a broader process of capital accumulation and industrialization. Both the tenant farmer and the landowner would have had an interest in increasing production for the domestic and export markets to make more profit and accumulate more capital. For the tenant farmer, higher crop yields and revenues would have required the introduction of better tools and equipment in the production process, in other words, labor-saving technologies; and for the landowner it would have meant raising the rents to the tenant farmers. As Brenner and Wood argue in chapter 1, the transformation of the tenant farmers into capitalists in their own right in England facilitated the further development of agriculture and industries in the seventeenth century.

That alternative never materialized in Haiti. One reason was that the sharecroppers and those small peasants with access to land would have needed to be expropriated to create a larger farming population without access to land alongside those who were already landless and hired themselves out as day laborers. Another factor against the introduction of more advanced labor-saving technology was the relatively small size and noncontiguous or fragmented configuration of the farms. Farmland, in other words, would have needed to be consolidated to make the cost of producing and buying labor-saving technologies worthwhile, all of which would also have necessitated the expropriation of the small landowners/possessors especially.

Achieving these transformations in turn would have necessitated a relatively stable government capable of planning, legislating, and investing public resources and revenues to achieve these desired ends. As Robert Fatton put it, Haiti needed what he called an "integral state" that could

> organize both the political unity of the different factions of the ruling class and the "organic relations between political society and civil society." It contains social conflicts within constitutional limits and manages processes of class formation, struggles, and compromises. Ultimately, it expresses the hegemonic governance of the ruling class—the capacity to command effectively without permanent resort to brute force. (Fatton 2007, 82)

Without such an "integral state," Fatton goes on to say, "politics tends to become predatory and chaotic" as well as despotic (2007, 83). Trouillot makes the same point when he argues that given the fundamental weakness of the state, "the governments that succeeded each other and were expressions of that state were necessarily authoritarian, for they had to use repression to check the civil society that they were unable to control through persuasion" (Trouillot 1990, 71).

Both Fatton and Trouillot drew on the Gramscian concept of hegemony, by which he meant that masses give consent to the "general direction imposed on social life by the dominant fundamental group [because of] the prestige and consequent confidence which the dominant group enjoys because of its position and function in the world of production." But he also points out that the "apparatus of state coercive power which 'legally' enforces discipline on those groups who do not 'consent' either actively or passively is, however, constituted for the whole of society in anticipation of moments of crisis of command and direction when spontaneous consent has failed" (Gramsci 1971, 12). Put differently, the state reserves the prerogative to silence or crush dissent and those who do not "agree" or "consent" to the rule of the dominant classes, which was the situation that prevailed in Haiti.

Democracy is first and foremost a matter of power, class power in particular. It is an expression of the "balance of power among different *classes and class coalitions* complemented by two other power configurations—the structure, strength, and autonomy of the *state apparatus* and its interaction with civil society and the impact of *transnational power relations* on both the balance of class power and on state-civil society relations" (Rueschemeyer et al. 1992, 5, emphasis in original). If that is the case, then, it cannot be argued, as Barrington Moore did for example, that the rise of modern capitalism, especially the "taming of the agrarian sector, [breaking] the political hegemony of the landed upper class, [turning] the peasant into a farmer producing for the market instead of for his own consumption, [and] disciplining the working class were decisive features of the whole historical process that produced such a [democratic] society" (B. Moore 1966, 429, brackets added).

Put differently, there is no necessary correlation between one's position in the class structures and production relations of any given capitalist society at any given point in time and one's proclivity toward democracy or dictatorship. This is so even if we limit the definition of democracy to its liberal or conventional variant: universal suffrage and the right to vote in regular, free, and fair elections of political representatives and heads of state; freedom of expression and assembly; the protection of individuals against arbitrary state actions; and freedom of private property ownership (Rueschemeyer et al. 1992, 43–44).

But even with this limited definition of democracy, which overlooks the fundamental issues of economic power, class exploitation, class domination, and the inequalities characteristic of capitalist society, it was not until the late nineteenth and for most of the twentieth century that universal suffrage was extended to all citizens regardless of race, gender, or property qualifications, in both the highly developed countries of the capitalist world economy (Britain, France, the Netherlands, Spain, Portugal, the United States, Canada), and the less developed parts of Latin/Central America and the Caribbean. As Wallerstein noted, the "history of the expansion of suffrage was always the result of a political struggle. And we see also that the widening of suffrage tended to be a concession by those in power to movements conducted by those who lacked the suffrage" (2003, 154). At the same time, as the uneven history of democracy in western Europe, Latin/Central America, and the Caribbean in the nineteenth and twentieth centuries has shown, capitalists can promote liberal democracy and oppose it in favor of fascism or dictatorship; or a major power intervenes militarily to overthrow or support the overthrow of an elected head of state it deems inimical to its interests. In that regard, the history of US interventions in this hemisphere and elsewhere throughout the twentieth century is well known and legendary. I therefore agree with Rueschemeyer, Stephens, and Stephens when they conclude in their comparative study of Latin America and the Caribbean that "capitalist development and democracy are related primarily through changes in the balance of class power. Yet our analyses also demonstrate that the level of democratic development cannot be simply read off from the level of capitalist development" (Rueschemeyer et al. 1992, 272).

The reason capitalism and democracy are not synonymous is that, as Wood puts it, the development of capitalism made it possible to decouple political rights from economic rights, that is, to construct a political sphere where citizens were formally equal but such an equality was not linked to "the inequalities of wealth and economic power outside the political domain." Henceforth, "political progress, or even the progress of democracy, could be conceived in terms that were socially indifferent, with an emphasis on political and civil rights that regulated the relations between citizens and state, not the maldistribution of social and economic power among citizens, who in the abstract sphere of politics were equal" (Wood 2012, 316).

In my view, then, Haiti's inability to create the democratic state that its many constitutions since independence (1805, 1806, 1807, 1811, 1816, 1843, 1846, 1867, 1874, 1879, 1888, 1889) proclaimed it to be was not an anomaly.

Such an outcome, that is, the extension of democratic rights (as described above) or its blockage, must be understood from the standpoint of the class structure, the balance of class forces, and the relations between them and the state in the context of its position in and interaction with foreign capital and powers in the capitalist world economy. But these struggles were not directly linked to, nor do they call into question—at least not yet—the capitalist structure of Haiti, its attendant social and economic inequalities, and its position in and relations with foreign powers and foreign capital in the larger capitalist world economy.

As a whole, the constitutions of Haiti in the nineteenth and up to the mid-twentieth century allowed for direct, popular, and universal elections of communal councilors and deputies to the national assembly, and the latter in turn elected the president. Presidents formed their own governments and chose their secretaries of state who, though not the president, were accountable to the Chamber of Deputies (the national assembly). The president also chose senators along with those chosen by the regional assemblies; and he appointed judges and government officials (Moïse 1988, 251–52). It was not until 1956 that direct, universal suffrage and elections for both the legislature and the presidency were achieved, leading Trouillot to observe that henceforth winning "control of the Legislature no longer guaranteed the outcome of presidential elections" (Trouillot 1990, 146).

As Moïse pointed out, however, although the parliament (Chamber of Deputies and Senate) passed laws and occasionally exercised some control over presidents throughout the nineteenth century, presidents who succeeded in controlling the military were also able to neutralize the powers and prerogatives of parliament such that its attempts to exercise its hegemony usually succumbed to the power plays of those presidents. Thus, between the "State to be constructed and the Nation to be consolidated the gap could not be filled" in the nineteenth century (Moïse 1988, 254). At the same time, as Fatton noted, "even if the autocrat has wide latitude to express his 'personal whims,' he is nonetheless subjected to his social base, which aspires to become a ruling class. In other words, the autocrat cannot escape being an element, albeit critical, in the wider process of class formation. He ultimately represents an ascending class in the making of a class seeking to preserve its dominant position" (Fatton 2007, 86).

Unlike other countries in Latin America and the Caribbean, Haiti's agrarian structure was not characterized by latifundia owned by a landed aristocracy and where the laborers were confined to them, as was the case on the slave plantations and briefly under Dessalines and Christophe. Boyer's attempt to re-create the plantation system and compel the laborers to live and work on them with his draconian 1826 *Code Rural* also failed, and was the last time such an attempt was made until the United States invaded and occupied Haiti from 1915 to 1934. This led to the landownership patterns, the agrarian system, and its attendant production relations and modes of surplus production and accumulation I described above. The key point here is that no matter whether they owned their own land or became tenant farmers or *métayers*, the peasant farmers produced most of their own food as well as food for the local/national markets and all the crops Haiti sold on the domestic and world markets. They were therefore commodity producers fully integrated in the circuits of global capitalism.

Second, the bourgeoisie in Haiti was unable to defeat the majority of the peasantry or expropriate and proletarianize them. This meant that it could not count on the state to offer the support that capitalist classes elsewhere usually rely on to develop a national infrastructure, expand public, technical, and professional education, diversify agriculture, and subsidize and promote the growth of small, medium-sized, and large industries. As a result, the Haitian bourgeoisie was stymied in its efforts or ability in the mid-nineteenth century to transform Haiti from a predominantly agricultural into a more industrial economy (Bellegarde 1938, 121–24; Dupuy 1989, 96–113; O. E. Moore 1972, 31; Turnier 1985, 211–18).

Given that to be the case, the dominant classes, especially but not exclusively the rural and the commercial bourgeoisie, were limited to accumulating wealth primarily from the circulation rather than directly from the production process. They became a rentier and a commercial bourgeoisie that engaged in rent extraction and in financial, commercial, and trade relations with other countries to which they could export Haiti's agricultural products, and from which they could import durable and consumer goods they resold on the domestic market.

In addition to commercial/urban-industrial, financial enterprises and/or land as the basis of wealth accumulation, the state and the prebends it yielded became a source of enrichment for those who controlled it.[15] Its bureaucratic, police, and military apparatuses also created their own system of clientelism and mechanism of wealth appropriation. Moreover, since the presidency also controlled the other branches of the state such as the legislature, the judiciary, and civil service bureaucracies in addition to the military and police, the tendency of those in power was to prolong their hold on that office as much as possible. Dictatorship and rule by force, then, became the only form of government possible under such circumstances, and coups d'état became the principal means of making and unmaking governments. That explains why between 1804 and 1915, out of the twenty-four heads of state in 111 years, thirteen were overthrown by force, three were killed while in office, six died in office, and two completed their terms (Dupuy 1989, 115–23).

The weakness, divisions, and endless conflicts among factions of the ruling class to control the state, fueled as they were by the racist ideologies of color, made them also vulnerable to manipulation and exploitation by foreign capital and their governments, and facilitated their dominance over the Haitian economy. Successive governments or would-be heads of state sought the support of foreign governments by making concessions to them and/or borrowing large sums of money from foreign banks. For example, President Fabre-Nicolas Geffrard (1859–1867) turned to England for its support against Sylvain Salnave, who was seeking to overthrow him. When Salnave succeeded and became president from 1867 to 1869, he offered to let the United States establish a naval station at the Môle Saint-Nicolas (on the northwest coast) in return for its support against Nissage Saget, who succeeded in overthrowing him. When Michel Domingue took power in 1874, he offered to let England establish a protectorate at the Môle in exchange for its support. When Lysius Salomon succeeded him in 1879 he promised the Môle along with the Île de la Tortue (off the north central coast) to the United States in return for its military support at the same time that he called on France to establish a protectorate over Haiti. President François Légitime, who lasted one year in office (1888–1889), was said to have offered the Môle to the French while Florvil Hyppolite, who overthrew Légitime and ruled for eight years (1888–1896), sought the support of the United States. No actual land concessions were ever made but heads or would-be heads of state used them as bargaining chips with foreign powers, all of which weakened them (Dupuy 1989, 126).

More serious and consequential than the never-materialized offers of territorial concessions, however, were the borrowings of large sums of money from foreign banks that opened the way for foreign capital to reassert its dominance over Haiti's economy. The most notorious of those financial transactions occurred with the so-called Domingue loan contracted with a French bank in 1874 for 15 million francs at 33 percent (meaning that Haiti received only 10 million). Unable to meet the two-year repayment terms, the Domingue government took out another loan for 50 million francs allegedly to consolidate the first loan with that of the "double" indemnity debt (the balance on which, in 1876, was 7.76 million francs with interest according to Turnier (1985, 27). In 1896, the government of T. Antoine Sam borrowed another 50 million francs, and again, with those loans not repaid, the government of Antoine Simon borrowed another 65 million francs at an annual rate of 5 percent to be paid in five years.

As Pierre-Charles summed it, between 1875 and 1910 Haiti borrowed a total of 166 million francs, "half of which were kept by the lenders under various pretexts. In all in 1914 Haiti's total foreign debt amounted to 113,156,500 francs. [And] it was not only foreign bankers who enriched themselves, but also many functionaries who confused the interests of the state with their own." These debts were not fully repaid until 1961 (Pierre-Charles 1967, 136–37). Moreover, it is worth noting the evolution of the ratio of these debts to Haiti's treasury, whose principal source of foreign currency came from its exports. According to Turnier, for every three dollars Haiti earned on its coffee exports in 1875, $0.33 went to service the foreign debt. That increased to $1.20 in 1896, and $1.00 in 1910 (Turnier 1985, 35). Looked at differently, the burden of repaying Haiti's foreign debts was not caused primarily by the indemnity but by subsequent debts accrued after 1875 for reasons other than repaying the indemnity when the ratio of the debt repayment rose from 11 percent of revenue before 1875 to 40 percent in 1875, and to 30 percent in 1910.

I agree with Péan, then, when he observed that as a result of these practices, the Haitian state became "a vulgar agent for the condottieri of international trade and finance" (Péan 2000, 266). It is worth noting here that Haiti was not unique in perfecting the art of corruption. As Wallerstein points out, it would be hard to find a government in the past century that has not engaged in corruption. Such practices as buying services or obtaining favorable decisions from politicians and public officials are endemic to capitalism. This is because while "capitalists operate via the market and wish governments to stay out of market operations, [in] practice, as every capitalist knows, the governments are crucial to their market success in multiple ways. No serious capitalist can afford to ignore governments, his own and those of any other country in which he operates" (2003, 152–53).

As Benoît Joachim noted, these onerous practices explain why none of the governments that succeeded Boyer sought to renegotiate or invalidate the indemnity, despite their criticisms of him for having agreed to this "shameful tribute." Instead, they all agreed to repay the indemnity, even at the cost of great difficulties not because they believed it was fair to indemnify the former colonialists, [but] to curry the favors of the French governments, and to live in peace with the France they all venerated. Because the interests [of the rulers of Haiti] did not coincide with those of the large majority of the nation, the ruling classes often gave in to the pressures exercised by the metropolitan rulers, even without any significant strengthening of relations between the two countries. (Joachim 1971, 364)

By the beginning of the twentieth century, and as a result of these self-serving political transactions, foreign banking capital had reestablished its control over the national economy, which in turn facilitated the return and dominance of foreign commercial and industrial capital. Laws that before 1843 protected the interests of Haitian merchants by limiting the rights and activities of foreigners—such as the prohibition against buying and owning real estate, limiting foreign trade to designated port cities, buying coffee and other crops only from Haitian merchants, buying and selling wholesale only, and paying high fees to trade—had since been gradually relaxed, changed, or not enforced. Once that happened, it was no longer just foreigners residing in Haiti and married to Haitians who could evade those restrictions. Foreign merchants now began to establish their businesses directly in Haiti and displace Haitians, even though that process was uneven and localized in certain port cities. These changes soon opened the way for direct foreign capital investment in production resulting from land concessions to European firms who began to produce and process coffee, cacao, vanilla, pineapples, rubber, and lumber. The US invasion and occupation of Haiti from 1915 to 1934 would complete that process. During and after the occupation, the Haitian currency, the *gourde*, would henceforth be pegged to the US dollar rather than the French franc; the United States became the single most important market for Haitian exports and imports and the unquestionably dominant political power broker in Haiti.

CONCLUSION

From the foregoing analysis, then, the following conclusions can be drawn. First, as I have shown, President Boyer, as was the case also for his predecessor Alexandre Pétion, did not offer to pay an indemnity to France because he/they feared French military aggression. They both knew that France was not preparing to or capable of sending a massive, Napoleonesque military expedition to reconquer its former colony at the time (1814–1838). Pétion and

Boyer did so instead to solve two problems simultaneously: to secure the recognition of Haiti's independence and to settle once and for all the property question in the interest of the Haitian ruling class as a whole, even if some may not have understood it as such. That is why no government since Boyer contested the legitimacy of the 1825 ordinance or the debts Haiti incurred to pay the indemnity. Former president Aristide was the only head of state to demand restitution from France for the indemnity on the grounds that France imposed the indemnity on his nineteenth-century predecessors and compelled Boyer to accept the ordinance or face military reprisals if he refused. As I have shown, however, that argument does not stand up to scrutiny. Pétion put that offer on the table first, and Boyer brought it to a conclusion. They both acted on their own agency, in the context of the respective domestic and international constraints they confronted, to advance what they believed to be in the interest of the nation they governed, but which also happened to coincide first and foremost with the interests of their class: the question of property.

Second, as onerous as it was for the treasury, the indemnity was not the principal cause of Haiti's inability to develop its economy in the nineteenth century. The key determining factors were, on the one hand, the inability of the Haitian ruling class to expropriate and proletarianize the former slaves and their descendants who had gained access to land of their own, revitalize the plantation system, and lay the ground for a more widespread infrastructural and industrial development, and, on the other hand, the internecine conflicts among different factions of the ruling class to control the apparatuses of the state as a means of enrichment through corruption and cronyism.[16] Those factors, I have shown, including how Haiti's rulers negotiated their relations with foreign powers and foreign capital, conditioned not only the relations between the dominant and subordinate classes in Haiti, but also Haiti's articulation with and function in the larger capitalist world economy and world market.

Third, the indemnity, and the moneys borrowed to repay it along with other loans incurred for different reasons, gave rise to nefarious practices among post-Boyer heads of state of borrowing more and larger sums of money from foreign bankers that increasingly taxed their ability to repay those debts. In addition to embezzling parts of those moneys for self-enrichment, these obligations weakened the governing classes and facilitated the return and dominance of foreign financial, commercial, and industrial capital, which in turn solidified Haiti's uneven development as a supplier of cheap labor and an exporter of agricultural crops, raw materials, manufactured goods, and, since the US occupation of 1915–1934, migrant labor. As Turnier summed it up succinctly: "To stop the descent into hell, goodwill, competence, and patriotism were not enough, and foreign aid was essential, whereas imperialism aimed to carve up its prey. External finance succeeded in transferring to the economy the colonialism that was politically defeated on the battlefields of Saint-Domingue, and thus perpetuate the past" (Turnier 1985, 40).

NOTES

1. Boyer was referring to unresolved negotiations that had been ongoing since 1814 when Pétion first raised the issue of paying an indemnity to compensate the former colonial property owners.

2. These instructions were contained in a letter the comte de Chabrol, the minister of marine and the colonies, gave to de Mackau before he left France (AP-1-20, 17 avril 1825).

3. After Boyer agreed to accept the ordinance, he proposed to send the sum of 1 million piastres to France as a down payment to show his intention to honor the indemnity. Inginac tried unsuccessfully to persuade him not to do that since nothing definitive had been concluded. And given that Haiti would need to borrow money in any case to start paying the indemnity, he argued, Haiti should negotiate with English and French banks to obtain the best offer and to deposit the million piastres, or more, in a European bank and use the interest it would yield to cover some of the costs of the indemnity. Boyer chose instead to borrow the money from a French bank, which Inginac thought was a costly mistake (Inginac 1843, 72). See note 11.

4. The Praslin uprising is so-called because it was planned on the Praslin plantation in the southwestern city of Les Cayes.

5. Much of the following section is derived from Dupuy 1989, 55–91.

6. Many functionaries and military officers took advantage of their positions to plunder the public treasury, steal the pay of soldiers, and dispossess citizens of their properties, among other forms of embezzlement. So widespread were these practices that Dessalines was said to have told his officials that they "could pluck the chicken but not to make it crow" (cited in Bellegarde 1938, 92).

7. In 1810, General André Rigaud returned to Haiti from France and was named general of division by Pétion. He subsequently tried to wrest control of the south from Pétion. Rigaud died in 1812, and General Borgella took control temporarily but submitted to Pétion's forces in 1812 (Ardouin 1958, 7:71–113).

8. There is some confusion on Medina's death. Wallez claims that he died in jail from illnesses. Ardouin and Madiou say he was killed (Wallez 1826, 16; Madiou 1988, 5:268; Ardouin 1958, 8:15).

9. By which Pétion meant the dispossessed colonial property owners.

10. Price-Mars realized that France was indeed bluffing by camouflaging its diplomatic maneuvers as coercive threats. This acknowledgment seems inconsistent with his subsequent claim that Boyer had capitulated to the threat of force when he agreed to pay the indemnity after he met with de Mackau.

11. Borrowing the money at 80 percent meant that Haiti received only 24 million francs, with the balance due in twenty-five years at 6 percent interest per year. This is why Inginac had advised him to negotiate with English and French banks to obtain a better and less costly deal.

12. The eastern Spanish colony was unified with Haiti from 1822 to 1843 under Boyer.

13. Vendryes was referring to the National Assembly that formed the first government of the French Revolution in 1789, and the National Convention that abolished slavery in 1794.

14. It is worth noting here, that in 1838 the French king acknowledged and contradicted what the Debray report hid behind cowardly to dismiss Aristide's demand for *restitution*, namely, the claim that the "rights of peoples to self-determination" was not recognized at the time. From my standpoint, however, Aristide's demand is unfounded not because it does not have legal standing but because it was offered as a *quid pro quo* by Pétion and seen through to its conclusion by Boyer in the interest of the Haitian bourgeoisie.

15. The term *prebend* is adapted from Max Weber, who used it to refer to those who hold public office "as a source of the official's private income." As he also put it, "prebends" or a "prebendal organization" refers to "the official rent payment for life, payments which are somehow fixed to the objects or which are essentially *economic* usufruct from land or other sources. They must be compensated for the fulfillment of actual or fictitious office duties; they are goods permanently set aside for the economic assurance of the office" (Weber 1946, 206–7). Weber formulated this concept of prebendal appropriation to analyze practices that originated in feudal societies, and especially in those societies like France and England where the purchase of office became institutionalized and continued into the early nineteenth century. I am using it here to describe how the holders of public office in Haiti, especially, but not limited to the executive branch of government, transformed those offices into sources of personal income and enrichment, thereby institutionalizing corruption as a form of prebendal income.

16. For the most comprehensive analysis of the "political economy of corruption" in Haiti, see Leslie Péan (2000, 2005, 2006, 2007).

Bibliography

ARCHIVAL AND CONTEMPORARY PRIMARY SOURCES AND ABBREVIATIONS

Archives Nationales, Paris, France

AE Fond Affaires Étrangères, Série B

Haïti: AE/B/III/380, 450, 458 (1818–1868)
AE-B-III-380 *Loi qui déclare dette nationale l'indemnité de 150,000,000 de francs accordée à la France, pour la reconnaissance de l'Indépendance d'Haïti*, 25 février 1826.
AE-B-III-458 Las Cases, Baron de. *Baron de Las Cases au Président Boyer*, 4 mars 1838.

Archives Nationales, Pierrefitte-sur-Seine, Paris, France

AP Archives Privées

AP-156-1-20. 18–38 (carrier); 40–53 (correspondence), Fonds Privés/Archives Privées: Archives de Mackau
AP-1-20. Comte de Chabrol. Comte de Chabrol au baron de Mackau, 17 avril 1825.
AP-1-20. *Ordonnance du Roi*, 17 avril 1825.
AP-1-20. *Extrait des articles additionnels secret du traité du 30 mai 1814.*
AP-1-20. de Mackau, baron. *Rapport à Son Excellence le Ministre de la Marine et des Colonies, de la Mission à Saint-Domingue de Mr. le baron de Mackau.* 7 juillet 1825.
AP-1-20. Boyer, Jean-Pierre. Boyer, au baron de Mackau, 8 juillet 1825.

ANOM Archives Nationale d'Outre-Mer, Aix-en-Provence, France

Fond des Colonies

Saint-Domingue: Série principale—Sous-série CC9A (1789–1850)
Mémoires, correspondances, rapports, documents divers concernant Saint-Domingue
CC9A-216 MIOM-34 *Article additionnel secret au traité conclu le 30 mai 1814 entre la France et la Grande Bretagne*, 24 juin 1814.
CC9A-48. *Rapport de Dauxion-Lavaisse à Malouet*, 1814.

MAE Ministère des Affaires Étrangères, Paris, France

(MAE-CP) Affaires Politiques/Correspondance Politique: Haïti 1816–1895. Vol. 1–11: 1816–1843.
MAE 47CP Haïti: v. 5, 1831–1832, *Le Télégraph*, 19 juin 1831.
MAE 47CP Haïti: v. 7, Las Cases, baron de. Lettre tout à fait pour l'histoire, 7 février 1838.
MAE 47CP Haïti: v. 8, *Ordonnance du Roi*, 30 mai 1838.

BNF Bibliothèque Nationale de France

Gallica Bibliothèque Numérique: gallica.bnf.fr

Dalloz, Désiré, Phillippe Dupin, J.-Elisabeth-Merthie, and Antoine Louis Marie Hennequin. 1829. *Consultation de MM. Dalloz, Delarange, Hennequin, Dupin jeune et autres jurisconsultes pour les anciens colons de Saint-Domingue*. Paris: Impremerie de Madame Veuve Agasse.

Doubs, Clément du. 1830. *Mémoire pour les Anciens Colons de Saint-Domingue: Au Roi, aux Chambres, à la France*. Paris: Imprimerie de A. Moreau.

Dubroca, L. 1802. *La vie de Toussaint Louverture, Chefs des noirs insurgés de Saint-Dominge*. Paris.

Du Tertre, R. P. 1667. *Histoire Générale des Antilles Habitées par les François, Tome II*. Paris: Thomas Iolly.

Esmangart, Charles. 1833. *La Vérité sur les Affaires d'Haïti*. Paris: Imprimerie de Carpentier-Mérucourt.

France. *Traité entre la France et les puissances alliées: conclu à Paris, le 20 Novembre 1815*.

Hilliard D'Auberteuil, Michel-René. 1776. *Considérations sur l'état présent de la colonie française de Saint-Domingue*, 2 vols. Paris: Grangé,. Manioc: Bibliothèque Numerique Amazonie Plateau des Guyanes.

Pièces officielles relatives aux négociations du gouvernement français avec le gouvernement Haïtien pour traiter de la formalité de la reconnaissance de l'indépendance d'Haïti, 1824.

Raimond, Julien. 1793. *Mémoire sur les causes des désastres de la colonie de Saint-Domingue*. Paris: Imprimerie du Cercle Social.

Vendryes, B. 1839. *De L'Indemnité de Saint-Domingue: considérée souls le rapport du droit des gens, du droit public des Français et de la dignité nationale*. Paris.

Wallez, Jean Baptiste Guislain. 1826. *Précis historique des négociations entre la France et Saint-Domingue*. Paris: Ponthieu.

CIAT Centre Interministériel d'Aménagement du Territoire, Port-au-Prince, Haiti

Ministère des Finances. 1834. *État Détaillé des Liquidations opérées pendant l'année 1832 et les six premiers mois de 1833.* Paris: Imprimerie Royale.

The National Archives, Kew, Richmond, England

FCO Foreign and Commonwealth Office Collection (1816)

Haiti and President (1807–1818): Pétion. *Piéces relatives à la correspondence de MM. les Commisaires de S. M. Très-Chrétienne et du Président d'Haïti.* University of Manchester, John Ryland University Library. Accessed February 20, 2014. http://www.jstor.org/stable/60234976.

University of Florida, Gainesville, Florida

Hérard, Charles. *Acte de Déchéance, au Nom du Peuple.* 10 mars 1843. http://ufdc.ufl.edu/UF00055543/00001.

Rochambeau Papers

Gambart. *Observations présentées au gouvernement sur l'administration générale de Saint-Domingue*, 27 Mars 1802.

Idlinger, Joseph Antoine. *Rapport sur la 4 ^{e} question qui m'à été faite aujourd'hui par le citoyen général en chef conçue en ces termes.* 3 Avril 1802.

Repussard, Faustin. "Lettre au Général de Division Rochambeau, 6 juin 1802." *Rochambeau Papers*. Gainsville: University of Florida.

USI Inquiry into Occupation and Administration of Haiti and Santo Domingo

Hearing before a Select Committee on Haiti and Santo Domingo, United States Senate, 67th Congress, First Session, August 5, 1921.

SECONDARY SOURCES

Adam, André Georges. 1982. *Une crise haïtienne 1867–1869: Sylvain Salnave.* Port-au-Prince: Henri Deschamps.

Adeeko, Adeleke. 2005. *The Slave's Rebellion: Literature, History, Orature.* Bloomington: Indiana University Press.

Anderson, Perry. 1984. "Modernity and Revolution." *New Left Review* 144 (March–April): 96–113.

Anievas, Alexander, and Kerem Nisancioglu. 2015. *How the West Came to Rule: The Geopolitical Origins of Capitalism.* London: Pluto.

Ardouin, Beaubrun. 1958. *Études sur l'Histoire d'Haïti.* 11 vols. 1853–1860. Port-au-Prince: F. Dalencourt.

Aristide, Jean-Bertrand. 2003, April 7. "Discours de Son Excellence Jean-Bertrand Aristide, Président de la République, à l'occasion de la Cérémonie Commémorative du Bicentenaire de la Mort de Toussaint Louverture." Port-au-Prince: Musée du Panthéon National.

Arrighi, Giovanni. 2001. *Adam Smith in Beijing: Lineages of the Twentieth Century.* London: Verso.

Auguste, Claude B., and Marcel B. Auguste. 1985. *L'expédition Leclerc 1801–1803.* Port-au-Prince: Henri Deschamps.

Barros, Jacques. 1984. *Haiti de 1804 à nos jours.* 2 vols. Paris: Éditions l'Harmattan.

Beauvois, Frédérique. 2009. "L'indemnité de Saint-Domingue: 'Dette d'independence' ou 'rançon de l'esclavage'?" *French Colonial History*, 10, 109–24.

Beckert, Sven. 2014. *Empire of Cotton: A Global History.* New York: Alfred A Knopf.

Behrendt, Stephen D., David Eltis, and David Richardson. 2001. "The Costs of Coercion: African Agency in the Pre-Modern Atlantic World." *Economic History Review* 54, no. 3 (August): 454–76.

Bellande, Alex, et al. 1980. *Espace rural et société agraire en transformation: des jardins haïtien aux marchés de Port-au-Prince.* Port-au-Prince: Institut Français d'Haïti.

Bellegarde, Dantès. 1938. *La nation haïtienne.* Paris: J. De Gigord.

Blackburn, Robin. 2011. *The American Crucible: Slavery, Emancipation and Human Rights.* London: Verso.

Blancpain, François. 2001. *Un siècle de relations financières entre Haïti et la France (1825–1922).* Paris: L'Harmattan.

Bogues, Anthony. 2010. *Empire of Liberty: Power, Desire, and Freedom.* Hanover, NH: University Press of New England.

Bonaparte, Napoléon. 1861. *Correspondance de Napoléon Ier. Tome Septième.* Paris: Henri Plon and J. Dumaine.

———. 1931. *Napoleon's Autobiography. The Personal Memoirs of Bonaparte Compiled from His Own Letters and Diaries by F. M. Kircheisen.* Translated by Frederick Collins. With an introduction by Henry Irving Brock. New York: Duffield & Company.

———. 1946. *Napoleon's Memoirs.* Edited by Somerset de Chair. London: Faber and Faber Limited.

Brenner, Robert. 1977. "The Origins of Capitalist Development: A Critique of Neo-Smithian Marxism." *New Left Review*, 104, 25–92.

Brière, Jean-François. 2008. *Haïti et la France 1804–1848: Le rêve brisé.* Paris: Editions Karthala.

Buck-Morss, Susan. 2009. *Hegel, Haiti, and Universal History.* Pittsburgh: University of Pittsburgh Press.

Burnard, Trevor, and John Garrigus. 2016. *The Plantation Machine: Atlantic Capitalism in French Saint-Domingue and British Jamaica.* Philadelphia: University of Pennsylvania Press.

Butler, Clark, and Christiane Seiler, trans. 1984. *Hegel: The Letters.* With commentary by Clark Butler. Bloomington: Indiana University Press.

Cabon, Adolphe. 1929. *Histoire d'Haïti.* 4 vols. Paris: Congrégation des Frères de Saint-Jacques.

Caroit, Jean-Michel. 2004. "Comment la France a préparé son retour en Haiti: Le rapport du comité présidé par Regis Debray preconisait une concertation avec Washington." *Le Monde*, April 15, 2004.

Célius, Carlo Avierl. 1997. "Le modèle social haïtien: Hypothèses, arguments et méthode." *Pouvoirs dans la Caraïbe*. Accessed October 15, 2015. http://plc.revues.org/738.

Césaire, Aimé. 1960. *Toussaint Louverture: La Révolution française et le problème colonial*. Paris: Livre Club Diderot.

Cheney, Paul. 2017. *Cul de Sac: Patrimony, Capitalism, and Slavery in French Saint-Domingue*. Chicago: University of Chicago Press.

Clarkson, Thomas. 1952. *Henry Christophe and Thomas Clarkson: A Correspondence*. Edited by Earl Leslie Griggs and Clifford H. Prator. Berkeley and Los Angeles: University of California Press.

Code Rural de Boyer 1826. 1992. Port-au-Prince: Archives Nationales d'Haïti and Henri Deschamps.

Cole, Hubert. 1967. *Christophe, King of Haiti*. New York: Viking.

Comay, Rebecca. 2010. *Mourning Sickness: Hegel and the French Revolution*. Stanford: Stanford University Press.

Coradin, Jean D. 1988. *Histoire Diplomatique d'Haïti 1804–1843*. Port-au-Prince: Edition des Antilles.

Cournand, Antoine de (Abbé). 1968. "Requête présentée à nosseigneurs de l'Assemblée Nationale en faveur des gens de couleur de l'île de Saint-Domingue, 1790." In *La Révolution française et l'abolition de l'esclavage. Vol 4: Traite des noirs et esclavage*. Paris: Éditions d'Histoire Sociale.

Curtin, Philip D. 1975. *Economic Change in Precolonial Africa: Senegambia in the Era of the Slave Trade*. Madison: University of Wisconsin Press.

Dartigue, Maurice. 1938. *Conditions Rurales en Haïti: Quelques donnés basées en partie sur l'étude de 884 familles*. Port-au-Prince: Imprimerie de l'état.

Davis, David Brion. 1975. *The Problem of Slavery in the Age of Revolution, 1770–1823*. Ithaca, NY: Cornell University Press.

Dayan, Joan. 1995. *Haiti, History, and the Gods*. Berkeley and Los Angeles: University of California Press.

Debien, Gabriel. 1945. *Comptes, profits, esclaves, et travaux de deux sucreries de Saint-Domingue, 1774–1798*. 2 vols. Port-au-Prince: Imprimerie Valcin.

———. 1950. "Gens de couleur et colons de St. Domingue." *Revue d'histoire de l'Amérique française*, no. 4.

———. 1962. "Plantations et esclaves à Saint-Domingue: Sucrerie Cotineau, 1750–77." *Notes d'Histoire Coloniale*, 66, 7–84.

Debray, Régis, et al. 2004. *Haïti et la France: Rapport à Dominique de Villepin, ministre des Affaires étrangères*. Paris: Éditions La Table Ronde.

Delince, Kern. 1994. *Quelle armée pour Haïti?* Paris: Karthala.

Desmangles, Leslie. 1992. *The Faces of the Gods: Vodou and Roman Catholicism in Haiti*. Chapel Hill: University of North Carolina Press.

De Vaissière, Pierre. 1909. *Saint-Domingue: La Société et la Vie Créoles sous l' Ancien Régime (1629–1789)*. Paris: Perrin.

D'Hondt, Jacques. 1989. "Le parcourt Hégélien de la Révolution française." *Bulletin de la Société française de philosophie* 83 (October–December): 115–30.

Dobb, Maurice. 1978a. "A Reply." In Rodney Hilton, ed., *The Transition from Feudalism to Capitalism*, 57–67. London: Verso.

———. 1978b. "A Further Comment." In Rodney Hilton, ed., *The Transition from Feudalism to Capitalism*, 98–101. London: Verso.

———. 1978c. "From Feudalism to Capitalism." In Rodney Hilton, ed., *The Transition from Feudalism to Capitalism*, 165–69. London: Verso.

Dorsinville, Luc. 1961. *Abregé d'histoire d'Haïti*. Port-au-Prince: Imprimerie de l'État.

Douglas, Paul H. 1927. "The Political History of the Occupation." In *Occupied Haiti*, edited by Emily Green Balch, 15–36. New York: The Writers Publishing Co., Inc.

Dubois, Laurant. 2004. *Avengers of the New World: The Story of the Haitian Revolution*. Cambridge, MA, and London: Harvard University Press.

Dupuy, Alex. 1976. "Spanish Colonialism and the Origin of Underdevelopment in Haiti." *Latin American Perspectives* 3 (2): 5–29.

———. 1981. *Feudalism and Slavery: Processes of Uneven Development in France and Saint-Domingue in the Eighteenth Century*. PhD dissertation. Department of Sociology, State University of New York at Binghamton.

———. 1989. *Haiti in the World Economy: Class, Race, and Underdevelopment since 1700*. Boulder, CO: Westview Press.

———. 2014. *Haiti: From Revolutionary Slaves to Powerless Citizens: Essays on the Politics and Economics of Underdevelopment, 1804–2013*. London and New York: Routledge.

Dupuy, Alex, and Paul Fitzgerald. 1977. "A Contribution to the Critique of the World-System Perspective." *Insurgent Sociologist* (Spring): 113–24.

Dye, Alan. 1998. *Cuban Sugar in the Age of Mass Production: Technology and the Economics of Sugar Central 1899–1929*. Stanford, CA: Stanford University Press.

Enzenberger, Hans Magnus. 1974. "Las Casas, or a Look Back into the Future." In *The Devastation of the Indies: A Brief Account*, edited by Bartolome de Las Casas. Translated by Herma Briffault. New York: Seabury Press.

Etienne, Eddy. 1982. *La vraie dimension de la politique extérieure des premiers gouvernements d'Haïti (1804–1843)*. Québec: Editions Naaman.

Eugène, Itazienne. 2003. "La normalization des relation franco-haïtiennes (1825–1838)." In Marcel Dorigny, ed., *Haïti: première république noire*, 139–54. Paris: Publications de la Société Française d'Histoire d'Outre-Mer, et Association pour l'Étude de la Colonisation Europeenne.

Fanon, Frantz. 1967. *Black Skin, White Masks*. Translated by Charles Lam Markmann. New York: Grove Press.

Farmer, Paul. 2003, November 3. "Douze points en faveur de la restitution à Haïti de la dette française." Institute for Justice and Democracy in Haiti. Accessed May 11, 2018. http://www.ijdh.org.

Fatton, Robert, Jr. 2007. *The Roots of Haitian Despotism*. Boulder, CO: Lynne Rienner.

Fauvelet de Bourrienne, Louis Antoine. 1895. *Memoirs of Napoleon Bonaparte*. Edited by R. W. Phipps. New York: Charles Scribner's Sons.

Ferrer, Ada. 2009. "Speaking of Haiti: Slavery, Revolution, and Freedom in Cuban Slaves Testimony." In *The World of the Haitian Revolution*, edited by David Patrick Geggus and Norman Fiering, 223–47. Bloomington and Indianapolis: Indiana University Press.

Fick, Carolyn E. 1990. *The Making of Haiti: The Saint-Domingue Revolution from Below*. Knoxville: University of Tennessee Press.

———. 1997. "The French Revolution in Saint-Domingue: A Triumph or a Failure?" In *A Turbulent Time: The French Revolution and the Greater Caribbean*, edited by David Barry Gaspar and David Patrick Geggus, 51–75. Bloomington and Indianapolis: Indiana University Press.

Fields, Barbara Jeanne. 1990. "Slavery, Race, and Ideology in the United States of America." *New Left Review* 181 (May–June): 95–118.

Fisher, Sibylle. 2004. *Modernity Disavowed: Haiti and the Cultures of Slavery in the Age of Revolution*. Durham, NC: Duke University Press.

Fouchard, Jean. 1953. *Les Marrons du Syllabaire*. Port-au-Prince: Henri Deschamps.

Frank, Andre Gunder. 1967. *Capitalism and Underdevelopment in Latin America: Historical Studies of Chile and Brazil*. New York: Monthly Review Press.

Franklin, James. 1828. *The Present State of Hayti (Saint-Domingue), with Remarks on Its Agriculture*. London: John Murray; rpt. Westport, CT: Negro University Press/Greenwood Press, 1970.

Friedman, Thomas L. 1998. "Foreign Affairs: Techno-Nothings." *New York Times*, April 18, 1998.

Garrigus, John D. 2006. *Before Haiti: Race and Citizenship in French Saint-Domingue*. New York: Palgrave Macmillan.

Geggus, David Patrick. 2002. *Haitian Revolutionary Studies*. Bloomington and Indianapolis: Indiana University Press.

Genovese, Eugene D. 1979. *From Rebellion to Revolution: Afro-American Slave Revolts in the Making of the Modern World*. Baton Rouge: Louisiana State University Press.

Gilroy, Paul. 1995. *The Black Atlantic: Modernity and Double Consciousness*. Cambridge, MA: Harvard University Press.

Girault, Christian A. 1981. *Le commerce du café en Haïti: Habitants, spéculateurs et exportateurs*. Paris: Editions de Centre National de la Recherche Scientifique.

Gisler, Antoine. 1965. *L'esclavage aux Antilles françaises, XVIIe-XIXe siècles*. Fribourg: Presses Universitaires Fribourg.

Gramsci, Antonio. 1971. *Selections from the Prison Notebooks of Antonio Gramsci*. Edited and translated by Quintin Hoare and Geoffrey Nowell Smith. London and New York: Lawrence & Wishart, and International Publishers.

Habermas, Jürgen. 1973. *Theory and Practice*. Translated by John Vierted. Boston: Beacon.

Hagelberg, G. B. 1985. "Sugar in the Caribbean: Turning Sunshine into Money." In *Caribbean Contours*, edited by Sidney Mintz and Sally Price, 85–126. Baltimore: Johns Hopkins University Press.

Hall, Gwendolyn Midlo. 1971. *Social Control in Slave Plantation-Society: A Comparison of Saint-Domingue and Cuba*. Baltimore: Johns Hopkins University Press.

Hall, Stuart. 1974. "Marx's Notes on Method: A 'Reading' of the '1857 Introduction.'" *Working Papers in Cultural Studies*, 6, 132–70.

Harris, H. S. 1979. "Hegel's System of Ethical Life: An Interpretation." In G. W. F. Hegel, *System of Ethical Life (1802/3) and First Philosophy of Spirit (Part III of the System of Speculative Philosophy 1803/4)*. Translated by H. S. Harris and T. M. Knox, 1–96. Albany: State University of New York.

Harvey, David. 2006. *Spaces of Global Capitalism: Towards a Theory of Uneven Geographical Development*. London: Verso.

Hector, Michel. 2009. "Problème du passage à la société postesclavagiste et postcoloniale (1791–1793/1820–1826)." In *Genese de l'Etat haitien (1804–1859)*, edited by Michel Hector and Laënnec Hurbon, 97–122. Port-au-Prince: Presses Nationales d'Haïti.

Hegel, G. W. F. 1956. *The Philosophy of History*. Translated by J. Sibree. New York: Dover.

———. 1967. *The Phenomenology of Mind*. Translated by J. B. Baillie. New York: Harper & Row.

———. 1975. *Lectures on the Philosophy of World History: Introduction: Reason in History*. Translated by H. B. Nisbet. Cambridge: Cambridge University Press.

———. 1976. *The Philosophy of Right*. Translated with notes by T. M. Knox. London: Oxford University Press.

———. 1978. *Philosophy of Subjective Spirit, Volume 2: Anthropology*. Translated by M. J. Petry. Dordrecht, Netherlands: D. Reidel Publishing Co.

———. 1979. *System of Ethical Life (1802/3) and First Philosophy of Spirit (Part III of the System of Speculative Philosophy 1803/4)*. Translated by H. S. Harris and T. M. Knox, 1–96. Albany: State University of New York.

———. 2007. *Lectures on the Philosophy of Spirit 1827–28*. Translated and with an introduction by Robert R. Williams. Oxford: Oxford University Press.

Hilton, Rodney H., ed. 1978. *The Transition from Feudalism to Capitalism*. London: Verso.

Honneth, Alex. 1995. *The Struggle for Recognition: The Moral Grammar of Social Conflicts*. Translated by Joel Anderson. Cambridge: Polity Press.

Hurbon, Laënnec. 2009. "Les religions dans la construction de l'État (1801–1859)." In *Genèse de l'État haïtien (1804–1859)*, edited by Michel Hector and Laënnec Hurbon, 189–202. Port-au-Prince: Presses Nationales d'Haiti.

Hume, David. 1742. *Essays and Treatises on Several Subjects*. 2 vols. Dublin: J. Williams.

Inginac, Joseph-Baltazar. 1843. *Mémoires de Joseph Balzar Inginac*. Kingston: J. R. De Cordova.

James, C. L. R. 1963. *The Black Jacobins: Toussaint Louverture and the San Domingo Revolution*. New York: Vintage.

Janvier, Louis-Joseph. 1886. *Les Constitutions d'Haiti (1801–1885)*. Paris: C. Marpon & E. Flammarion.

Jean-Baptiste, Saint-Victor. 1957. *Hait, sa lutte pour l'émacipation: Deux concepts d'indépendance à Saint-Domingue*. Paris: Éditions Nef de Paris.

Jefferson, Thomas. 1984. "Notes on the State of Virginia." In Thomas Jefferson, *Writings*, 123–325. New York: Library Classics of the United States.

Joachim, Benoît. 1971. "L'indemnité de Saint-Domingue et la question des rapatriés." *Revue Historique* 246 (October–December): 359–76.

———. 1979. *Les racines du sous-développement en Haiti*. Port-au-Prince: Imprimerie H. Deschamps.

Johnson, Ronald Angelo. 2014. *Diplomacy in Black and White: John Adams, Toussaint Louverture, and Their Atlantic World Alliance*. Athens: The University of Georgia Press.

Kant, Immanuel. 1799. *Essays and Treatises on Moral, Political, Religious, and Various Philosophical Subjects*. Vol. 2. London: William Richardson.

Knight, Franklin. 1978. *The Caribbean: The Genesis of a Fragmented Nationalism*. Oxford and New York: Oxford University Press.

Kojève, Alexandre. 1969. *Introduction to the Reading of Hegel: Lectures on the Phenomenology of Spirit*. Translated by James H. Nichols Jr. New York and London: Basic Books.

Labelle, Micheline. 1978. *Idéologie de couleur et classes sociales en Haïti*. Montréal: Les Presses de l'Université de Montréal.

Lacroix, François-Joseph Pamphile, baron de. 1820. *Mémoires pour servir à l'histoire de la révolution de Saint-Domingue*. 2 vols. Paris: Pillet Ainé.

Las Casas, Bartolome de. 1974. *The Devastation of the Indies: A Brief Account*. Translated by Herma Briffault. New York: Seabury Press.

Laurent, Gérard M. n.d. *Six études sur Jean-Jacques Dessalines*. Port-au-Prince: Imprimerie Les Presses Libres.

Léger, Abel-Nicolas. 1930. *Histoire Diplomatique d'Haïti*. Tome premier (1804–1859). Port-au-Prince: Imprimerie A. Héraux.

Léger, J. N. 1907. *Haïti, son histoire et ses détracteurs*. New York: Neale Publishing.

Le Noir de Rouvray, Laurent-François. 1959. *Une correspondance familiale au temps des troubles de Saint-Domingue: Lettres du Marquis et de la Marquise de Rouvray à leur fille, Saint-Domingue-Etats-Unis, 1791–1796*. Edited by M. E. McIntosh and B. C. Weber. Paris: Société de l'Histoire des Colonies Françaises et Librairie Larose.

Léon, Pierre. 1963. *Marchands et spéculateurs dauphinoise dans le monde antillais du XIIIe siècle*. Paris: Les Belles Lettres.

Léopold-Hector, Marion. 1977. "La résistance paysanne en Haïti: éléments pour une analyse." Série G. Working Papers no. 9, University of Ottawa: Institute for International Co-operation, March 1977.

Lewis, Gordon K. 1983. *Main Currents in Caribbean Thought: The Historical Evolution of Caribbean Society in Its Ideological Aspects, 1492–1900*. Baltimore: Johns Hopkins University Press.

Leyburn, James G. 1941. *The Haitian People*. New Haven, CT: Yale University Press.

Liedman, Sven-Eric. 1976. *A World to Win: The Life and Work of Karl Marx*. London: Verso.

Luc, Jean. 1976. *Structure économique et lutte nationale populaire en Haïti*. Montréal: Les Éditions Nouvelle Optique.

Lundahl, Matts. 1979. *Peasants and Poverty: A Study of Haiti*. New York: St. Martin's.

Madiou, Thomas. 1988. *Histoire d'Haïti*. 7 vols. Port-au-Prince: Editions Fardin.

Malik, Kenan. 1996. *The Meaning of Race: Race, History and Culture in Western Society*. New York: New York University Press.

Manigat, Leslie. 1962. *La politique agraire du gouvernement d'Alexandre Pétion*. Port-au-Prince: Imprimerie La Phalange.

Martinez, Samuel. 1995. *Peripheral Migrants: Haitians and Dominican Republic Sugar Plantations*. Knoxville: University of Tennessee Press.

Marx, Karl. 1973. *Grundrisse: Foundations of the Critique of Political Economy*. Translated by Martin Nicolaus. Harmondsworth: Penguin.

———. 1975. "Economic and Philosophic Manuscripts of 1844. In Karl Marx and Frederick Engels, *Collected Works, V. 3: Marx and Engels: 1843–44*, 229–346. New York: International Publishers.

———., 1976. *Capital: A Critique of Political Economy, Volume One*. Introduced by Ernest Mandel and translated by Ben Fowkes. London: Penguin.

———. 1977. "Critique of the Gotha Programme." In *Karl Marx: Selected Writings*, edited by David McLellan, 564–70. Oxford and New York: Oxford University Press.

Mathon, Alix. 1985. *Haïti, un cas*. Port-au-Prince: Imprimerie Le Natal.

Mbeki, Thabo. 2004. "Address by the President of South Africa, Thabo Mbeki, at the Celebrations of the Bicentenary of the Independence of Haiti." Port-au-Prince, Haiti, January 1, 2004.

Mbembe, Achille. 2017. *Critique of Black Reason*. Translated by Laurent Dubois. Durham: Duke University Press.

Métral, Antoine. 1818. *Histoire de l'Insurrection des esclaves dans le Nord de Saint-Domingue*. Paris: F. Scherff.

Midy, Franklin. 2009. "Marrons de la liberté, révoltés de la liberation: Le Marron inconnu revisité." In *Genèse de l'État haïtien (1804–1859)*, edited by Michel Hector and Laënnec Hurbon, 123–48. Port-au-Prince: Éditions Presses Nationales d'Haiti.

Millet, Kethly. 1978. *Les paysans haïtiens et l'occupation américaine, 1915–1930.* Québec: Collectif Paroles.

Mintz, Sidney W. 1974. *Caribbean Transformations*. Chicago: Aldine.

———. 1977. "The So-Called World System: Local Initiative and Local Response." *Dialectical Anthropology* 4 (November): 253–70.

———. 1978. "Was the Plantation Slave a Proletarian?" *Review* 2 (Summer): 81–98.

———. 1985. *Sweetness and Power: The Place of Sugar in Modern History*. New York: Viking.

Moïse, Claude. 1988. *Constitutions et luttes de pouvoir en Hait (1804–1915), Tome I: La Faillite des Classes Dirigeantes*. Montréal: Les éditions du CIDIHCA.

Montague, Ludwell Lee. 1940. *Haiti and the United States 1714–1938*. Durham, NC: Duke University Press.

Montesquieu, Charles de Secondat, Baron de. 1973. *De l'Esprit des lois*. 2 vols. Introduction by Robert Derathé. Paris: Éditions Garnier Frères.

Moore, Barrington, Jr. 1966. *Social Origins of Dictatorship and Democracy: Lord and Peasants in the Making of the Modern World*. Boston: Beacon.

Moore, O. Ernest. 1972. *Haiti: Its Stagnant Society and Shackled Economy*. New York: Exposition.

Moral, Paul. 1961. *Le paysan haïtien: Étude sur la vie rurale en Haïti*. Paris: G. P. Maisonneuve et Larose.

Moreau de Saint-Méry, Médéric-Louis-Elie. 1797. *Description topographique, physique, civile, politique et historique de la partie française de l'Île de Saint-Domingue*. 3 vols. Paris: Dupont; rpt. Société de l'Histoire des Colonies Françaises et Librairie Larose, 1958.

Moreno Fraginals, Manuel. 1976. *The Sugar Mill: The Socio-economic Complex in Cuba*. Translated by Cedric Belfrage. New York: Monthly Review Press.

———. 1985. "Plantations in the Caribbean: Cuba, Puerto-Rico, and the Dominican Republic in the Late Nineteenth Century." In *Between Slavery and Free Labor: The Spanish-Speaking Caribbean in the Nineteenth Century*, edited by Manuel Moreno Fraginals, Frank Moya Pons, and Stanley L. Engerman, 3–21. Baltimore: Johns Hopkins University Press.

Mousnier, Roland. 1965. *Histoire générale des civilisations, vol. 4: Les XVIe et XVIIe siècles*. Paris: Presses Universitaires de France.

Moya Pons, Frank. 1998. *The Dominican Republic: A National History*. Princeton, NJ: Marcus Wiener.

Nau, Emile. 1894. *Histoire des Caciques d'Haïti*. Paris: Gustave Guerin et Cie.

Neptune Anglade, Mireille. 1986. *L'autre moitié du développement: à propos de travail des femmes en Haïti*. Port-au-Prince: Éditions des Alizés and Montreal: Études et recherches critiques d'espace.

Nesbitt, Nick. 2004. "Troping Toussaint, Reading Revolution." *Research in African Literature* 35, no. 2 (Summer): 18–33.

Nicholls, David. 1979. *From Dessalines to Duvalier: Race, Colour and National Independence in Haiti*. New York and London: Cambridge University Press.

Outlaw, Lucius. 1990. "African Philosophy: Deconstructive and Reconstructive Challenges." In *Sage Philosophy: Indigenous Thinkers and Modern Debate on African Philosophy*, edited by H. Odera Oruka, 223–48. Leiden and New York: E. J. Brill.

Parkin, Frank. 1979. *Marxism and Class Theory: A Bourgeois Critique*. New York: Columbia University Press.

Parry, J. H. 1967. "Transport and Trade Routes." In *The Cambridge Economic History of Europe, Vol. 4: The Economy of Expanding Europe in the Sixteenth and Seventeenth Centuries*, edited by E. E. Rich and C. H. Wilson, 155–219. Cambridge: Cambridge University Press.

Patterson, Orlando. 1982. *Slavery and Social Death: A Comparative Study*. Cambridge, MA: Harvard University Press.

Péan, Leslie. 2000. *Haïti: Économie politique de la corruption: De Saint-Domingue à Haïti, 1791–1870*. Paris: Maisonneuve et Larose.

———. 2005. *Haïti: Économie politique de la corruption: L'État marron (1870–1915)*. Tome II. Paris: Maisonneuve et Larose.

———. 2006. *Haïti: Économie politique de la corruption: Le saccage.* Tome III. Paris: Maisonneuve et Larose.

———. 2007. *Haïti: Économie politique de la corruption: L'ensauvagement macoute et ses conséquences 1957–1990.* Tome IV. Paris: Maisonneuve et Larose.

Phillips, Anthony D. 2009. "Haiti's Independence Debt and Prospects for Restitution." Institute for Justice and Democracy in Haiti. Accessed May 11, 2018. http://www.ijde.org.

Pierre-Charles, Gérard. 1967. *L'économie haïtienne et sa voie de dèveloppement.* Paris: Maisonneuve et Larose.

———. 1972. "Genèse des nations haïtienne et dominicaine." *Nouvelle Optique* 8 (October–November).

Pinkard, Terry. 2000. *Hegel: A Biography.* Cambridge: Cambridge University Press.

Placide, Justin. 1826. *Histoire politique et statistique de l'Ile d'Haïti, Saint-Domingue, écrite sur les documents officiels et des notes communiquées par sir James Barskett.* Paris: Brière.

Pluchon, Pierre. 1979. *Toussaint Louverture: de l'esclavage au pouvoir.* Paris: Éditions de l'École.

Plummer, Brenda Gayle. 1988. *Haiti and the Great Powers, 1902–1915.* Baton Rouge: Louisiana State University Press.

Pomeranz, Kenneth. 2000. *The Great Divergence: China, Europe, and the Making of the Modern World Economy.* Princeton, NJ: Princeton University Press.

Price-Mars, Jean. 2009. *La République d'Haïti et la République Dominicaine.* Tome 1. Port-au-Prince: Les Éditions Fardin.

Radio Métropole. 2003. "Réparations pour la dette de l'indépendance: le gouvernement français répond à M. Aristide." Port-au-Prince, Haiti, April 9, 2003.

Ramsey, Kate. 2011. *The Spirits and the Law: Vodou and Power in Haiti.* Chicago: University of Chicago Press.

Rauch, Leo. 1983. "Introduction: On Hegel's Concept of Spirit." In *Hegel and the Human Spirit: A Translation of the Jena Lectures on the Philosophy of Spirit (1805–6),* edited by Leo Rauch, 15–81. Detroit: Wayne State University Press.

Robinson, Randall. 2004. "Honor Haiti, Honor Ourselves, Forget Haiti, Forget Ourselves." *Counterpunch,* January 1, 2004.

Rueschemeyer, Dietrich, Evelyn Huber Stephens, and John. D. Stephens. 1992. *Capitalist Development and Democracy.* Chicago: University of Chicago Press.

Sala-Molin, Louis. 1987. *Le Code Noir ou le calvaire de Cannan.* Paris: Presses Universitaires de France.

Saint-Louis, Vertus. 2008. *Mer et liberté en Haïti (1492–1794).* Port-au-Prince: Bibliothèque Nationale de Haïti.

Saint-Rémy, Joseph. 1956. *Pétion et Haïti: Études monographique et historique.* 15 vols. 2nd ed. Paris: Librairie Berger-Levrault.

Sannon, H. Pauleus. 1933. *Histoire de Toussaint-Louverture.* 3 vols. Port-au-Prince: Imprimerie A. Héraux.

Sauer, Carl Ortwin. 1969. *The Spanish Main.* Berkeley: University of California Press.

Schoelcher, Victor. 1843. *Colonies Étrangères et Haïti, Résultats de l'émancipation anglaise.* Paris: Pagnerre, Éditeur.

———. 1889. *Vie de Toussaint Louverture.* 2nd ed. Paris: Paul Ollendorff.

Scott, Rebecca J. 1985. "Explaining Abolition: Contradictions, Adaptation, and Challenge in Cuban Slave Society, 1860–1886." In *Between Slavery and Free Labor: The Spanish-Speaking Caribbean in the Nineteenth Century,* edited by Manuel Moreno Fraginals, Frank Moya Pons, and Stanley L. Engerman, 25–53. Baltimore: Johns Hopkins University Press.

Smith, Adam. 1998. *An Inquiry into the Nature and Causes of the Wealth of Nations: A Selected Edition.* Oxford and New York: Oxford University Press.

Soboul, Alfred. 1989. *The French Revolution 1789–1799: From the Storming of the Bastille to Napoleon.* Translated by Alan Forrest and Colin Jones. London: Unwin Hyman.

Sweezy, Paul. 1978a. "A Critique." In Rodney Hilton, ed., *The Transition from Feudalism to Capitalism*, 33–56. London: Verso.

———. 1978b. "A Rejoinder." In Rodney Hilton, ed., *The Transition from Feudalism to Capitalism*, 102–8. London: Verso.

Tavares, Pierre-Franklin. 1992. "Hegel et Haiti, ou le silence de Hegel sur Saint-Domingue." *Chemins Critiques* 2, no. 3 (May): 113–31.

Thomas, Clive Y. 1988. *Power and the Powerless: Economic Policy and Change in the Caribbean.* New York: Monthly Review Press.

Thompson, Alvin. 1998. "The Berbice Revolt, 1763–64." *Themes in African-Guyanese History*, 77–105.

Thornton, John. 1998. *Africa and Africans in the Making of the Atlantic World, 1400–1800.* Cambridge: Cambridge University Press.

Tibebu, Teshale. 2011. *Hegel and the Third World: The Making of Eurocentrism in World History.* Syracuse: Syracuse University Press.

Tomich, Dale W. 2004. *Through the Prism of Slavery: Labor, Capital, and World Economy.* Lanham, MD: Rowman & Littlefield.

———. 2008. "Thinking the 'Unthinkable': Victor Schoelcher and Haiti." *Review: Fernand Braudel Center for the Study of Economies, Historical Systems, and Civilizations* 31 (3): 401–31.

Toussaint, Eddy (Tontongi). 2010, August 30. "La France doit restituer à Haïti la rançon de l'indemnité." *AlterPresse.*

Trouillot, Michel-Rolph. 1977. *Ti Difé Boulé sou istoua ayiti.* Brooklyn, NY: Koleksion Lakansiel.

———. 1990. *Haiti: State against Nation.* New York: Monthly Review Press.

———. 1991. "From Planters' Journals to Academia: The Haitian Revolution as Unthinkable History." *The Journal of Caribbean History*, 25, 81–99.

———. 1995. *Silencing the Past: Power and the Production of History.* Boston: Beacon.

Turnier, Alain. 1985. *La Société des Baïonnettes.* Port-au-Prince: Imprimerie Le Natal.

Vendryes, B. 1839. *De L'Indemnité de Saint-Domingue.* Paris: Chez l'Auteur.

Voltaire, François-Marie Arouet. 1963. *Essai sur les mœurs et l'esprit des nations.* Edited with an introduction and notes by René Pomeau. Paris: Éditions Garnier Frères.

Walker, Andrew. 2019. "All Spirits Are Roused: The 1822 Anti-Slavery Revolution in Haitian Santo Domingo." *Slavery and Abolition: A Journal of Slavery and Post-Slavery Studies.* https://doi.org/10.1080/014439X.2019.1565438. Accessed February 25, 2019.

Wallerstein, Immanuel. 1974. *The Modern World-System, I: Capitalist Agriculture and the Origins of the European World-Economy.* New York: Academic Press.

———. 1976. "The Rise and Future Demise of the World-Capitalist System: Concepts for Comparative Analysis." In *The Capitalist World-Economy: Essays by Immanuel Wallerstein*, 1–36. Cambridge: Cambridge University Press.

———. 2003. *The Decline of America Power: The U.S. in a Changing World.* New York and London: New Press.

Wallez, Jean-Baptiste Guislain. 1826. *Précis Historique des Négociations entre la France et Saint-Domingue.* Paris: Ponthieu.

Weber, Max. 1946. *From Max Weber: Essays in Sociology.* Translated, edited, and with an introduction by H. H. Gerth and C. Wright Mills. New York: Oxford University Press.

Williams, Eric. 1966. *Capitalism and Slavery*. New York: Capricorn.

———. 1970. *From Columbus to Castro: The History of the Caribbean 1492–1969*. New York: Harper & Row.

Wood, Ellen Meiksins. 2002. *The Origin of Capitalism: A Longer View*. London: Verso.

———. 2003. *Empire of Capital*. London: Verso.

———. 2012. *Liberty and Property: A Social History of Western Political Thought from Renaissance to Enlightenment*. London: Verso.

Index

About the Author

Alex Dupuy is John E. Andrus Professor of Sociology Emeritus at Wesleyan University in Middletown, Connecticut. He is an internationally recognized scholar and specialist on Haiti. He has lectured at universities and colleges across the United States and abroad and has given many interviews and commentaries on Haitian affairs on local, national, and international radio and television networks, including the *PBS NewsHour*, Toronto Public TV, *Democracy Now!*, WBAI, National Public Radio, Pacifica Radio, the BBC, the CBC, Radio France International, and the Australian Broadcasting Company. In addition to his many articles in professional journals and anthologies, he is the author of *Haiti in the World Economy: Class, Race, and Underdevelopment since 1700* (1987); *Haiti in the New World Order: The Limits of the Democratic Revolution* (1997); *The Prophet and Power: Jean-Bertrand Aristide, the International Community, and Haiti* (2007); and *Haiti: From Revolutionary Slaves to Powerless Citizens—Essays on the Politics and Economics of Underdevelopment (1804–2013)* (2014).